THE BOOK

of ARTS

AND CRAFTS

Marguerite Ickis *and* Reba Selden Esh

D0067079

Dover Publications, Inc.
New York

Published in Canada by General Publishing Company, Ltd., 30 Lesmill Road, Don Mills, Toronto, Ontario.
Published in the United Kingdom by Constable and Company, Ltd., 10 Orange Street, London W. C. 2.

This Dover edition, first published in 1965, is an unabridged and unaltered republication of the work first published by the Association Press in 1954.
The illustrations in this book are by Reba Selden Esh.

International Standard Book Number: 0-486-21472-9

Library of Congress Catalog Card Number: 65-24025

Manufactured in the United States of America

Dover Publications, Inc.
180 Varick Street
New York, N. Y. 10014

Contents

THE BOOK OF ARTS AND CRAFTS

1

Introduction to Arts and Crafts

The crafts described in this book are based on human needs. These are divided into five groups—home, personal adornment, camps and playgrounds, little children, and special crafts for the individual. One of the most important needs in the craft field is for projects that can be used for therapy. Almost any craft in the book can be used for this purpose, and the occupational therapist can adapt it to fit the needs of his program.

This book should be particularly helpful to the beginner in crafts or the group leader as well as the experienced craftsman who is looking for new ideas for things to make. Although over one thousand projects have been developed, we hope they will be used only as examples from which hundreds of other craft articles will be created in the craftsman's own form and design. Each project is intended to teach a basic technique which may be adapted to various needs. Many of the projects utilize scrap materials.

We have endeavored to prove that a creative craft program can be planned so that each project may be executed with little or no cost and with the use of simple tools.

Each craft is fully described and the directions for making it can be easily followed. The major mediums—wood, leather, metal, plastics, paper, textiles, and clay—are developed, giving basic techniques used in developing these materials.

This book is dedicated to the teachers, recreation leaders, therapists, and homemakers who desire a creative craft program involving a minimum of equipment and cost. We hope they will find many helpful suggestions in the following sections.

CREATIVE VALUE OF LEISURE TIME

The machine age has brought a revolution to both labor and leisure. Now there are many less hours of labor and many more of leisure. The tensions which result from production lines and similar ways of living must be relieved by something more creative than passive rest. The choice lies with the person, for he may experiment with music, drama, art, nature, and crafts. Frequently these are so integrated that all of them are found in a single activity.

Since handicrafts play so useful a part in recreation of any kind, it is important to know the primary skills involved in working with the various materials and their possible uses in other activities. The projects here are planned to illustrate the integration of a craft in other fields of interest. No craft is considered as an end in itself. A puppet and a stage without a play are incomplete and do not serve their full purpose.

Crafts made from materials which are available in the community are valuable to playground leaders, camp counselors, church group leaders, and school teachers. Natural materials are an example.

Natural Materials in Creative Activity

The question frequently asked by a novice craftsman is "Where do we get material and what does it cost?" The reeds, grasses, vines, shells, wood, and other things that grow provide a wealth of material and cost only the effort to collect them. Good taste in the selection and use of them determines their value. They may be combined with materials which are bought commercially. The tools are those to be found in any household.

Home Furnishings Is a Craft

Modern architecture, which plans a house to fit its location, its owner, his needs and personal tastes, is opening the way for creative furnishings. An imaginative wood worker builds tables and cupboards that need not be like any his neighbors have. His requirements and his ideas of function decide the form of the finished articles, and he can make them in his own shop.

Personal Adornment

Many people never try to make anything for themselves or their friends. "I am just not gifted that way," they say. Again the commercialization of clothes and accessories is the real reason. As more children are educated in our modern schools where individuality is stressed, the urge to make their own personal belongings will increase.

4

CARE AND PREPARATION OF MATERIAL

The care and preparation of material must be carefully considered, both by the teacher and the individual craftsman. First of all, a good storage room or closet is essential. Collecting materials is a continuous process if the budget is to be kept at a low level. It is expensive to go out and buy every item as you need it, so you store for a rainy day. Everything must be stored properly or it will be wasted—worst of all, you are not able to find it.

There are many places where useful and excellent materials can be found. Make the rounds of stores that throw away packing materials. You may find pieces of thin wood, cardboard in color, or strips of metal. Merchandise packed in foreign countries often yields new types of wood and woven straw packing. The paper might also make attractive lamp shades. Once you get started, your enthusiasm will carry you to the tinsmith, lumberyard, shoemaker, and even beyond to the factory.

If you are collecting pieces of wood, separate them according to hard or soft quality. Keep a bin for odd-shaped pieces. Be sure the wood is well dried or seasoned before piling it away; otherwise, it will warp or become mildewed. Lay wood on a flat surface, but never lay it directly on a floor if there is a chance that it will become damp.

Clay will keep indefinitely if placed in an airtight container. A large crock with a tight-fitting lid is best for this purpose. Inspect the clay from time to time and add more water if it becomes dry. It is a good idea to cover the clay with a wet cloth before sealing it with a lid.

All metals should be carefully stored with layers of paper or cardboard between the sheets. This will prevent scratches—which would require buffing in the finished article. Be sure to store away all scraps which may be used for jewelry at a later date.

Plastics, of course, are soft and easily scratched. Both sides of the surface must be covered with paper, even while work on the article takes place. Plastics come in many interesting forms such as tubes, strips, and blocks. Hollow tubes in various sizes can be purchased for making rings, beads, or bracelets.

It is most important to store leather in such a manner that it will not become creased or the surface scratched. Large pieces should be rolled and placed carefully on a shelf where nothing can fall on them. Small pieces should be smoothed out and laid perfectly flat.

These few suggestions should get you started with your supply room. Just remember, a craftsman should always collect materials as they turn up—he never knows when a use will come along.

HAND TANNED LEATHER

OLD TANNERY, BUNKERTOWN, PA.

HEAVY BARRELS

FLESHING KNIFE

SHAVER

SLICKER

STONE

HIDE ON LOG

HAND TANNED LEATHER

Tanning of animal skins was one of man's earliest crafts. The skin was preserved so that he might use it for clothing, shelter, and utensils. Sometimes the hair was kept on the hide but usually it was removed.

Through the centuries the process has changed from the primitive method of salting, drying, and manipulating the hide to soften it. The work was carried on in the tribes or families until tanning followed other home crafts and became a commercial industry. Tanneries were built where water power was available to turn the large water wheels. These turned the grinders to grind the tan bark and furnished water for the pumps to carry the tanning liquor through the vats where the hides were cured for almost a year. Now this method of tanning is being replaced by more modern ways, but for home craft the way to be described is most suitable.

The tannery shown at the top of the illustration has been dismantled recently after serving for over a century. Modern methods have replaced much of the hand work which was done there, but the quality of the leather has not been replaced. Many a leather craftsman will miss the texture and pungent odor of the hand tanned leather and be willing to improvise ways of making it.

The eighty-year-old tanner of Bunkertown has done this. He secured three heavy barrels to substitute for the vats where the hides were soaked. To explain his "modern method," he took the writer through his old tannery and explained each step of the old process as he had practiced it. "Tanning is very simple," he said, "but it takes time and hard work."

According to his explanation, a heavy steer required a year or more but a calf or deer hide may be made into leather in eight or nine months. Hides are secured from farmers, butchers, or at slaughter houses and should be used as soon as possible after their removal from the animal.

First, the hide is soaked in lime water made of thirty pounds of slacked lime and ten gallons of water. This requires from four to twelve hours. After this the hair is loose and it, together with any flesh which is on the inside of the hide, is scraped off with a dull knife. To do this, the skin is spread over a curved surface—and the aged tanner led the way to a smooth peeled log where he had scraped the hides. He took what he called a fleshing knife and after turning it over, removed the flesh from the inside. He cautioned about cutting the skin, to avoid holes in the finished leather.

When the hair and flesh are removed, the skin is next immersed in the tanning "liquor." "Use weak liquor first," he said. The liquor is a solution of water and oak bark, made by using about five pounds of bark to each gallon of water. When asked about the grinding of the bark, he led the way to an ancient grinder which stood on the porch of the tannery. As a substitute for the ground bark he would now use "extract," which he buys commercially, but the bark can be ground at a paper mill. A really enthusiastic craftsman could get one of these old grinders and operate it with an electric motor, and would find it worth his while. The oak bark is peeled from live oak trees in the spring when the sap is rising.

The old tanner continued his description of the early process and led the writer to three large vats which were built in the ground. They were still full of the oak "liquor," as he called it. The first contained the weakest solution and the other two were progressively stronger. "Leave the hides in the weak liquor about a month," he said, "and then move them into the second vat. After two or three months move them into the last one." He said that they should stay here for the remainder of the time. "Of course," he said, with a half-sad smile, "I use barrels now."

From here he went to his substitute vats, which were the three oak barrels filled with the varying solutions. They made the same process possible if only two or three small skins were to be tanned. One steer hide could be tanned in the barrels.

When the hide is sufficiently tanned it is removed and allowed to dry, and here is where the work really begins. Again the hide is scraped with a shaver to give it a more uniform thickness and finish. Dubbin—to use the tanner's terminology—is rubbed into the hide as it is worked. This softens the leather. The dubbin is a combination of equal parts of neat's-foot oil and tallow. After the shaving, a further finish is added by rubbing the leather with a smooth stone.

Although most of the leather at the tannery was light tan, some of it was black. This is done by applying a solution made by soaking scraps of iron and copperas in some of the tanning liquid. Copperas is crystallized ferrous sulphate, $FeSO_47H_2O$. Before putting this on the hide, the area is washed with water and household soda and allowed to dry. The dye is patted on with a cloth and when the color has penetrated about one-half the thickness of the leather, dubbin is rubbed on to stop the dye from going deeper.

A final polish with the stone, and the fine leather will repay the year of work and care.

SPINNING

The flax wheel so frequently found in homes furnished in the colonial tradition is a symbol of an almost forgotten home craft. Learning to spin was as much a part of a housewife's accomplishments as her cooking or sewing. She spun linen and woolen yarn for the clothing of the family. The woolen yarn was sometimes spun on a larger wheel, but the smaller flax wheel was commonly used. Although modern industry has replaced them with spinning machines, the delightful texture of fabric woven from homespun yarn has never been duplicated.

Learning to spin is not difficult and the woolen yarn or linen thread is beautiful when woven into rugs, woolen upholstery material, or linen cloth.

To begin with, you must find a complete spinning wheel. If there is one available with parts missing, a woodworker can replace them. Figures 1 and 2 show a complete wheel and a detail drawing of the spindle, which is the piece most likely to have been broken or lost. Check the wheel for the treadle, spindle, and belt. This belt is a continuous cord which fits into the grooves on the large wheel and through both grooves on the spindle. It goes twice around the large wheel.

For learning, wool is easier to handle. A fleece is the wool as it is clipped from the sheep or goat. It may be spun as it is—without washing—and thus retain the lanolin or natural grease, but it is more pleasant to handle when clean.

To wash wool, use lukewarm water and as little soap as possible. Four or five changes of water are usually sufficient. Squeezing the wool in the hands is the best way to remove the water. Avoid tangling it and do not attempt to wash it in a washing machine. It is usually advisable to do small quantities at a time. A piece of chicken wire makes a good frame to spread the wool on for drying.

When the wool is dry, pull it apart as much as possible with the fingers and remove sticks and burs. The next process is called carding. Cards (Fig. 3) are available at mail-order companies. Carding is done by taking a card in each hand, placing a small amount of wool on one, and pulling the other card across it until the fibers are untangled. By slightly rolling it when finished, a batt is formed and it is ready for spinning unless you decide to dye the wool before it is spun.

By dyeing the wool before spinning, two or three colors may be carded together, providing a greater variety of colors and mixtures. While learning, it is well to use the natural color because it takes

9

SPINNING

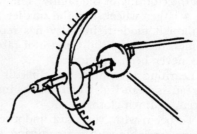

FIG. 1
FLAX
WHEEL.
WOOL AS
WELL AS
LINEN IS SPUN

DETAIL OF SPINDLE
AND THREADING "EYE"
AND CONTINUOUS BELT
FIG. 2

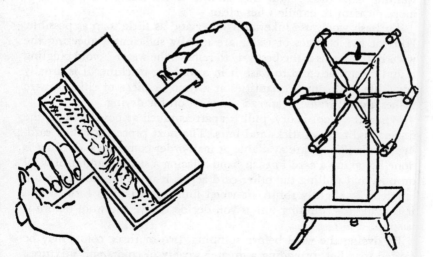

FIG. 3 CARDING WOOL

FIG. 4 REEL

several attempts before "good" yarn is made and some wool will be lost.

When the batts are made, the next step is to learn to treadle the wheel steadily. Next, tie a foot or two of string to the spool in the spindle, run it across one of the hooks on the spreader and out through the hole in the end of the spindle which is toward you. Take a batt of wool in your right hand—if you are right-handed—and the string in your left. Twist the two together slightly, transfer this to the left hand and as you start to treadle with the right foot give the larger wheel a slight turn to the right with the right hand by touching the wheel. When it starts, return the batt to the right hand and use the left as a guide on the yarn just in front of where the wool is twisting onto the thread now being formed. Keep the left hand about 6" from the end of the spindle at first, and as you become more skillful, move back until there is a foot or more of yarn between the spindle and the left hand. Use the right hand to hold the batt and to gauge the amount of wool being played out to the spindle. When there is about an inch of the batt left in your hand, stop the wheel, lay a new batt on the remaining batt—thinning the new one slightly at the jointure—and continue as you began. To spread the yarn evenly over the spool, move the thread across the hooks on the spreader.

If the yarn breaks and needs to be threaded through the hole again, twist the yarn tightly and double a loop which will be easily pushed through the "eye."

All of this takes patience and determination. At first the yarn will probably be lumpy and uneven, but it is surprising how soon beautiful smooth fine yarn will be coming from your fingers.

When the spool is full, the yarn is removed by slipping the belt out of the groove in the first pulley of the spindle. Wind the yarn into a ball or if you have a reel, attach the yarn to it and wind it into a skein (Fig. 4).

This is one ply yarn. If double ply is desired, it is made by allowing two strands to twist together. Make the single ply yarn into two balls. Lay them in your lap; put an end of each through the eye of the spindle and draw them back on the spool by treading the wheel.

Another slower way, but making less twist in the yarn, is to make the yarn into two balls and twist the two together as they are rolled into a single ball. The yarn is smoother if it is made into a skein, wet, and hung on a hook with a weight fastened to the lower end of the skein until it is dry.

HOW TO RECLAIM CLAY

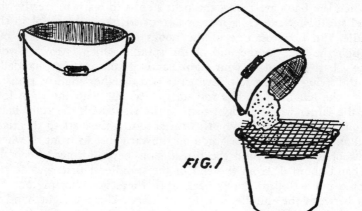

FIG. 1

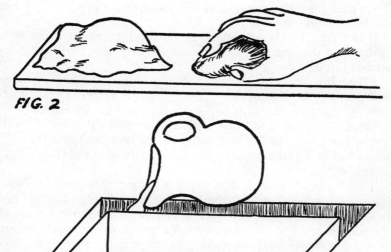

FIG. 2

FIG. 3

HOW TO RECLAIM CLAY

Clay beds are found along river banks in many localities throughout the country, and very often the clay is suitable for modeling or making pottery. If you can locate some natural clay, take a small quantity at first and prepare it for use. Refine it by removing all foreign material and send a sample away to be fired. To refine the clay, proceed as follows:

Place a quantity of clay in a bucket and cover it with several inches of water. Allow it to stand until the clay is dissolved to form a thick liquid called slip. Pour this through a sieve into another container to strain out large particles and small stones (Fig. 1). Set the container aside until all clay settles to the bottom. Drain off all water, then allow it to stand several days until the extra water evaporates.

The clay is now ready to have the air bubbles or pockets removed. This is called wedging. It is done by throwing chunks on a hard surface over and over, or by kneading with the hands (Fig. 2). The clay is now ready to be molded. When perfectly dry, a sample may be fired.

Clay that has been modeled but not fired may be reclaimed in the same manner. If clay is to be used for fine pottery, it should be run through a sieve each time it is reclaimed. It should be stored in an airtight container when not in use, preferably a stone jar, or a plastic bag.

One of the problems in reclaiming natural clay is the length of time it takes to dry out after it has been refined. If you are working with a group at camp you might make a plaster of Paris vat in which to dump the clay after extra water has been removed. The porous walls will allow the water to seep out and you will not need to wait until it evaporates. To do this, dig a pit 14″ deep and as large as you need. Cover the bottom with 2 inches of plaster. Make a double wall around the pit with heavy cardboard or wood. Set the walls several inches apart to form a mold for foundation. Pour in the plaster of Paris, as shown in Figure 3. Remove the walls when plaster is dry.

NATURAL DYES

Coloring of craft materials at home is done with dyes you prepare from leaves, roots, and flowers or with commercial dyes. The advantage in making dyes, aside from the pleasure of experimenting, is that unusual colors can be made. By combining or overdyeing, colors are harmonized and matched to furniture upholstery, draperies, and clothing.

There are a few things you must know if you are to be successful in using dyes. You mix a mordant—a chemical which prepares the textile to take and hold dye. Some dyes are successful on both wool and cotton, but wool takes and holds more kinds of dye. To mordant one pound of wool, use ¼ ounce of alum and 1 ounce cream of tartar. Put the wet wool in a solution of this and four gallons of cold water. Bring it to a boil and boil it gently for one hour. Let the wool cool in the water, rinse it, and it is ready for the dye. To mordant one pound of cotton, use 4 ounces alum and 1 ounce of washing soda. Follow the same directions as for the wool.

This chart shows how some colors are made:

Color	Material	Mordant	Time	Ingredient	Dyeing Time
Red	Wool	Alum and cream of tartar	1 hr.	8 oz. madder, soak 8 hrs. Boil in 1 qt. water	45 min. in 4 gal. liquid
Red	Cotton	Alum and washing soda	1 hr.	same as red wool	45 min. in 4 gal. fluid
Yellow	Wool	Alum and cream of tartar	30 min.	¾ peck zinnia petals and heads. Boil in 1 gal. water 10–15 min. Strain	Boil 30 min. in 4 gal. water
Yellow	Cotton	Alum and washing soda	Follow instructions for yellow on wool.		
Blue	Wool or Cotton	No mordant		4½ oz. powdered indigo, 3 oz. sodium hydroxide, 2¾ oz. sodium hydrosulphite	30 min. in 4 gal. fluid. Hang in air 30 min. and dip again
Brown	Wool or Cotton	No mordant		¾ peck green black walnut hulls. Boil 15 min. Strain	20 min. in 4 gal. fluid

For orange, overdye red with yellow.
For green, overdye yellow with blue.
For violet, overdye red with blue.
Overdyeing means dyeing the material the first color, letting it dry, and then using the second color.

THE CARE OF ART MATERIALS

Art materials are frequently used in making a craft article. We will describe some of these materials and their proper use. The "adding of color" to a craft material means that paint or dye is to be applied to it.

There are three basic kinds of color. All paints are minute particles of pigment held together with a binding element. The binders are water, oil, alcohol, or a solution combining these. The water-bound are dry tempera, dyes, water-color cakes or tubes, and some kinds of printing ink. Those mixed with oil are oil paint in tubes or cans, dry paint or tempera in oil, and printing ink. The oil is usually linseed. The third group, with alcohol, are usually commercial mixtures and frequently use only the solvent which comes with them. Colored ink and textile paints are examples. Any mixture which includes shellac contains alcohol.

Brushes and containers used for any of these are cleaned with the binding solution of the paint. Soap and warm water are used as a final cleanser for all of them. Brushes which present the most difficult problem become no problem if they are cleaned each time they are used. The bristles or hair will remain serviceable until they are worn out if they are dried in their proper shape. This assures not only serviceability but clean, clear color the next time they are used.

Paint containers should be kept closed tightly. A coating of oil on the contents of the can prevents a crust forming on it. Water-color sets should have each cake cleaned after use to assure clear color for the next project. Liquid tempera hardens in the jar if air reaches it, and becomes useless. The same is true of liquid textile colors. Commercial dyes, which usually come in paper envelopes, are kept in a dry place to avoid hardening. They can be dissolved but there is danger of little bumps which cause uneven results when used.

The care of art materials becomes easy if everything is clean and the paints are kept in airtight containers.

DESIGN IN CRAFTS

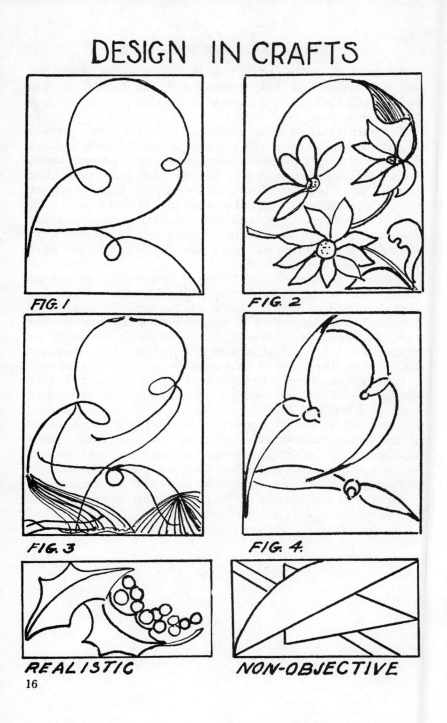

FIG. 1

FIG. 2

FIG. 3

FIG. 4

REALISTIC

NON-OBJECTIVE

DESIGN IN CRAFTS

All crafts have a design—the way they are put together and the decorations which are applied to them. Certain elements govern design, and how they are combined makes a good craft or an unsatisfactory one.

The first element, called function, reflects the purpose for which the object is intended. To achieve this, suitable material and mechanical efficiency in the working parts are necessary. The second is beauty, which evolves from the way the material is handled. To secure beauty, designers employ balance, rhythm, and contrast in materials in applied designs. Applied design is usually understood to be decoration, which in turn is governed by the use for which the craft is intended.

When a leatherworker plans a wallet, he knows that it will carry cards and money of certain dimensions. He plans the size of the wallet accordingly. He is concerned with safety for the contents and convenience in the arrangement of the inside sections. He uses materials which will wear well. This is the functional side of his craft. He may be satisfied with the texture of the material and fine workmanship to provide enough beauty. He may decide to go on and apply some additional decoration. Again function enters, for the decoration should suit the material and not decrease its efficiency.

Design in Decoration

Decoration is acquired by two processes. The one is integration, where the decoration is worked into the craft as it is being made. The other is added to the surface when it is partly or altogether finished. In weaving, knitting, inlaying of wood, and similar projects the decoration is made as the work progresses. Painting, embroidering, tooling, and etching are applied to the surface of the material being used.

What is decoration? It is a quest for beauty beyond the function of the craft. Variety, balance, and rhythm are its guides. How is decoration planned? Again the material is the deciding factor. For a craft where fibers are being woven to make the textile, various colors or textures of the material are arranged to make stripes or bars. They are placed to secure balance and variety. When the decoration is to be applied to the material as in painted designs, the pattern is usually drawn first, transferred, and colored. This is also true of embroidery.

Design for Young or Old Beginners

Use a pencil and paper. Cut the paper the size of the space to be decorated. For a first trial start without a plan and allow your natural sense of direction to lead your hand in making a series of lines. Do not make too many lines.

Figure 1 shows what can be made from a few lines. In this drawing the lines formed three circles, which the artist visualized as the centers of flowers. The other lines he used as stems (Fig. 2). Another artist interpreted the same circles as the heads of dancers and used the remaining lines as arms and legs (Fig. 3). Still another's interpretation of this same series of lines used the small circles as heads of flying birds. The lines alone could be used for a decoration.

Now look at the lines you have drawn and see how many different patterns can be made from them. Try this with several sets of lines. Next, using pencil and paper, mark off a space as large as the space you wish to decorate. Use the same method of putting the lines in it. Perhaps these lines will be sufficient as they are, but make several sets of lines on extra paper. Select the one you feel is most pleasing and apply it to your craft.

Other ways to secure decorative designs are traditional stencils and traced or copied pictures. Be sure to try to make your own and the satisfaction of an original design will add to your pride in the craft.

Design According to the Rules

A designer who wishes to work according to the accepted laws of design must consider arrangement, which is controlled by balance, contrast, and rhythm.

Balance is compared to a set of scales or a seesaw. If the board of the seesaw is horizontal with equal weights on each end, it is perfectly balanced but nothing is happening and it is uninteresting. If the one end is up and the other is on the ground, the observer is waiting for the reversal of the order and thus his interest is held. Balance in a design simply means that each part of the surface expresses equal weight, but this must be achieved without monotony. Some parts may be small and heavy or bright, while others, to keep the balance, are large and light or dull. This adds contrast. By such a combination some parts of the design are emphasized. Rhythm is shown in the way the eyes are led from one part of the arrangement to another part. It is said to be successful when all parts of the design are included in this visual tour.

2

Crafts in the Home

Since the "usefulness" of an article is one of the best measuring sticks for judging a good craft, making something for the home is a good beginning. The project you select may be utilities, such as utensils, dishes, kitchen accessories, or it may be draperies, bedspreads, or vases that will add decoration to your home.

It is a sad commentary that American homes are supplied almost entirely with machine-made merchandise and the folk crafts of earlier days have disappeared from the scene. To appreciate handwork one needs only to compare a handmade quilt with thousands of tiny stitches and a beautiful quilted pattern with those purchased at a store. The same comparison can be made of articles made of wood, metal, clay, or other mediums. The creating of such projects allows the individual to express his own personality.

A home workshop is an excellent device for bringing the family unit together. If you haven't a room that can be set aside for this purpose, select a corner with a storage cupboard where materials and tools may be kept. Each member of the family should be allowed to pursue his own interest or hobby, but occasionally a family should plan a co-operative project for the home. The work can be shared by father doing the cutting and assembling, small children smoothing parts with sandpaper, and a talented member adding a decoration.

A home workshop should be carefully planned and added to over a long period of years. It can be enjoyed as a relaxation from the tension of our highly mechanized living, as a source of additional income in producing salable crafts, and even as a business after retirement from your present occupation.

WOOD PROJECTS

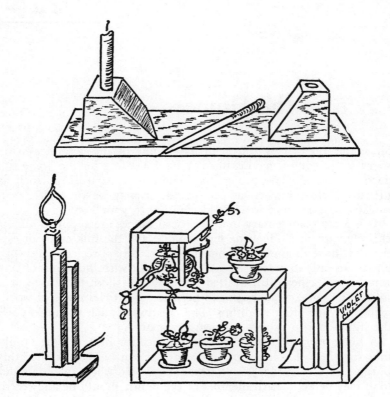

PIG
STOOL

WOODWORKING

Small wood projects such as those illustrated on the opposite page are excellent for the beginner. To begin with, you will need an old table for a workbench, wood, drill, a coping saw, saw blades, steel square, sandpaper, and a hammer and nails. These are essential working tools, and others can be added as you discover a need for them.

How to Cut Wood. Small pieces of wood are usually cut with a coping saw. This type of saw is used for cutting around curves as well as for making cutouts in the center of a piece of wood. Trace on the wood the design you wish to cut and drill a hole at a point on the edge of the design. The hole is for inserting the saw blade, so should be 1/8" in diameter. Fasten the blade in top of the saw frame, draw the blade down through the hole in the wood, and attach to the bottom of the frame. Be sure the points on the blade point away from the frame.

Begin working the saw up and down and saw in an outward direction. When you are ready to turn a curve, move the saw up and down several times without pressure on the blade and then saw in the regular manner. When the cutting is completed, loosen the blade from the bottom of the frame and remove the blade.

Use a hand saw for cutting straight lines or larger pieces of wood. Be sure to buy a saw that has 12 teeth to an inch; otherwise, it is hard to push up and down.

How to Join Wood. If wood is to be joined, sand the edges until they are smooth. Be sure the edges are even and fit exactly together. Put glue on the edges and set the two ends in place. To make the joining more secure, drive in a number of finishing nails. Force the nails a little below the surface and fill the hole with plastic wood. After the wood is joined and the glue is dry, smooth the edges again with a plane or sandpaper.

How to Finish Wood. Smooth the wood with several grades of sandpaper, ending with the finest. Next, put on a coat of wood filler and smooth again. At this point you must decide whether you want to add a stain or finish in the natural color. If you want a natural finish, add a coat of shellac or clear varnish. Allow to dry, and rub it down with fine steel wool or fine sandpaper. If you want a hard, lasting finish, repeat this process several times. Finally, add a coat or two of wax and rub thoroughly with a soft rag.

How to Stain Wood. Commercial wood stains in all colors can be purchased at a hardware store. However, it is possible to mix your own stain by dissolving oil paints in turpentine. A mixture of burnt umber and burnt sienna makes a beautiful color for lamps or furniture. Squeeze some oil paint from a tube into a bowl and add about a cup of turpentine. Stir the mixture until it is dissolved and rub some on a scrap piece of wood. If the color is too light, add more paint; or lighten the color by adding more turpentine. Apply the stain by dipping a cloth into the mixture and rubbing it over the wood. Keep adding a little turpentine as you go along, because the stain tends to become darker. Allow the stain to dry and then add a coat of clear varnish or shellac. Rub this down thoroughly with fine steel wool or sandpaper and then add another coat. Complete the finish by rubbing again and add a coat of wax.

Handmade Furniture

To make your own furniture you will need to add a few new tools to your collection. They are a sanding machine, chisels, a large woodworking vise and clamps. Secure a plane to which joining tools can be added for making grooves and other wood cuts. It is also a good idea to make a mitre box for cutting angles.

Select only good grade lumber for making furniture. The first step is to make a detailed drawing of the object you want to make and to figure the amount of lumber you will need. If you want to use a soft wood, pine, poplar, or redwood are most commonly used. The poplar wood has grain running through it which makes it more decorative when a natural finish is desired. Most popular of the hard woods are maple, cherry, walnut, and mahogany.

The cutting of the wood is most important. The measurements must be exact; otherwise, short pieces will have to be discarded and ones too long shortened. It is advisable to cut all major pieces before joining together, in order to assemble them to see if they fit and if your drawing is correct.

Join the pieces by putting glue on the edges, and then strengthen by adding a number of finishing nails. Since the nails are headless, force them a little below the surface and fill the hole with plastic wood.

After the pieces are joined, the surface must be thoroughly sanded. Finish the surface by adding paint, or give it a natural finish.

HUTCH TABLE

The hutch table was used in early American homes, but it serves especially well in small modern houses because it doubles as a table when needed and a seat at other times. The base has a hinged lid under which there is storage space. Three loose wooden pins hold the top in place when it is used as a table, and the two back pins form a hinge when it is used as a seat.

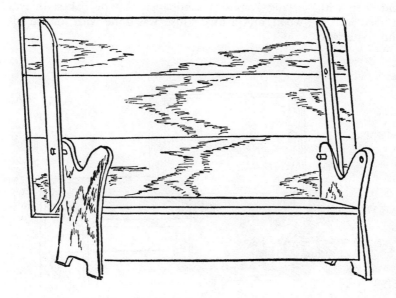

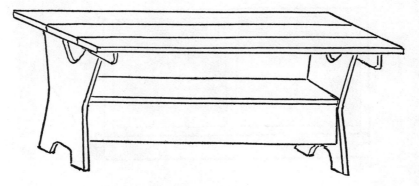

RECORD CABINET

The cabinet below is designed to hold record albums in the lower sections. There is room for the player on top. At the side is a framework in which a small radio fits. One inch clear pine was used for the cabinet. The base is 32″ long, 14½″ wide, and 19″ high. Plywood was used for the back. The holder for the radio is 14″ long, 9″ wide, and 9″ high. Small dowels give support at the front corners. All of the edges are rounded with a wood rasp, smoothed first with a file and then with varying grades of sandpaper. A pale oak stain was rubbed into the wood, and a final finish was done with linseed oil and paste wax.

PAINTED FURNITURE

"Folk Art" is the art of people who without formal training in the fine arts decorate their furniture, their homes, and handicrafts. They make the things they need and because they enjoy doing it, the results are usually fine. Museums throughout the world contain evidence of the skill, pride, and genuine good taste of these artisans.

For the person who feels the urge to paint but has had little opportunity to do so, freehand painting on furniture is a good place to begin. You may use a motif that is pictorial or related to nature, such as a fish, butterfly, flower, bird, or leaf; or use anything else you choose. There are certain brush strokes that may help you get started or improve your method of painting if you have some experience. These have been selected from peasant art of several countries. Oil paints are used and when they are dry, a coat of clear varnish is brushed over the work. This kind of painting would well suit some of the furniture described in "New Furniture from Old," pages 50–51.

Frequently, a piece of furniture with drawers and shelves is no longer in fashion and ugly in its present form. By removing the doors from a cupboard, adding a new cornice and interesting designs, it becomes useful and attractive. Old dressers, beds, desks, large tables, with a little carpenter work and paint can be transformed.

After the carpenter work is completed, you should sand the wood or paint enough to smooth it but it is not necessary to remove the old finish. Apply two coats of flat paint first and let them dry. Draw your designs and paint them with oil paints. When dry, several finishes may be used depending on the color of the first coat. If it is white, burnt umber thinned with turpentine is rubbed over the background and toned down with a cloth to give what is called an antique effect. Gold radiator paint may be used in the same way. Silver or gold over black, dark blue, or red is also effective. Rub most of the umber, gold, or silver off, leaving just enough to be seen. When this is dry, cover the whole piece with clear varnish. Deck varnish or other waterproof varnish should be used on surfaces exposed to much wear.

PAINTED FURNITURE

BRUSH STROKES

WORKING WITH METAL

Since we are concerned in this book with crafts that require few tools and equipment, we can only give you some basic facts and a few techniques about metal to get you started. Copper is popular with the craftsman because of its workable qualities and rich color. Pewter is also good, particularly for making plates, bowls, and other tableware. Aluminum is sometimes used in craft shops where budgets are low and there are many children hoping to learn metalcraft.

All metals come in sheets in different thicknesses known as "gauges." The metals used by a craftsman generally run anywhere from 14 to 36 gauge. A 36 gauge metal is almost as thin as paper; the 14 gauge is the thickest and is used for making trays and other large articles.

How to Cut Metal

Make a paper pattern of the article you wish to make and trace the outline on the metal. Fasten the metal in a vise so the area that is to be cut extends beyond the table. Cut around the edge with a jeweler's saw. After the cutout is completed, file away the slivers and smooth the edges with emery paper. You are now ready to shape the article.

How to Shape Metal

Metal is first blocked or domed, then raised, and finally planished. Blocking is done in a wooden mold or on a sandbag with a wooden or rawhide mallet. If the head of the mallet becomes marred, cover the ends with scrap leather. Begin the shaping by pounding around the outer rim and gradually working toward the center. The object is then raised to the shape desired. This can be done by turning it over on a stake and pounding it with a wooden or metal hammer. This technique helps to remove any kinks and folds that have formed in the hollow mold. Finally the planishing can be done. This is an all-over design of small markings made by striking blows with a planishing hammer. It gives a final shape and finished appearance to the object. If thick copper is used, it will have to be annealed between processes because the metal hardens from the hammer blows. Annealing means softening the metal over a flame by making it red-hot and then immersing in a bath of sulphuric acid pickle, followed by washing in warm water. In mixing acid always start with the water and add the acid very slowly.

Polishing Metal

After an article is completed, it must be cleaned and polished. The first step is to rub it thoroughly with fine steel wool. Remove

METAL

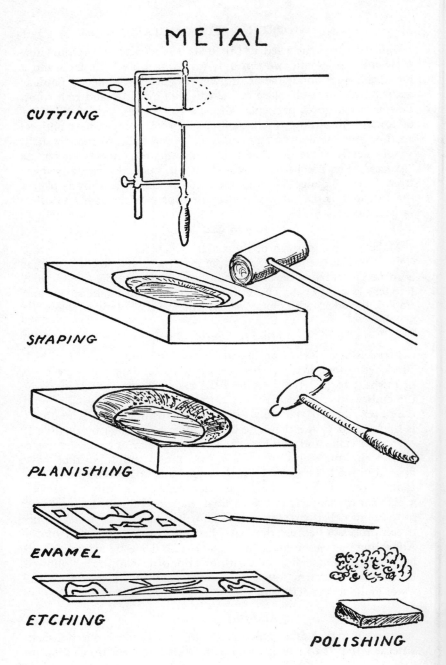

CUTTING

SHAPING

PLANISHING

ENAMEL

ETCHING

POLISHING

all scratches with wet emery paper. The final finish is done on a buffing machine. If you do not have one, rub some jeweler's rouge on a soft cloth and rub by hand.

How to Decorate Metal

Metals can be chased by incising the surface with dies and stamps. This raises or lowers the surface. A spike can be utilized on soft metals. Metal can be pierced by drilling holes and then cutting the design out with a jeweler's saw. Enameled designs can be painted on the metal if color is desired.

Etching on Metal

Etching on metal is done by covering parts of the surface with an acid resistant and using an acid to eat away whatever parts are exposed. It works in varying degrees on copper, pewter, nickel, silver, or aluminum. The covered parts remain in relief while the exposed parts are lowered, depending on the time the acid is on the metal and the strength of the acid or etching fluid. You can paint on the design and lower the background, or paint around the design and expose it to the acid. Designs that are to be etched must be planned for brush application. Large areas and curved lines are best for the beginner. Small articles such as trays, bracelets, and pins are suggested for the first projects.

A type of paint called asphaltum is used for protecting the metal from the acid. If you cannot purchase it at your local store, substitute liquid stove polish, which contains the same ingredients. Since the acid will eat away at any part of metal exposed, in the case of a flat object it is necessary to paint the back of it as well. If you are working with a group that must complete the painting in one period, ask that the back be painted first. Use a piece of wrapping paper and turn the metal over on it while the paint is still wet. The designs can then be painted and allowed to dry. Turn the paper close to the edge of the metal and let the paper remain while it is in the bath.

The painted articles should dry at least four hours before placing them in the acid bath. Straighten all edges around the design by removing extra paint with a small blade. Prepare the acid bath as follows: Use 2 parts water and 1 part nitric acid. Place the water in the pan first and then add the acid slowly. Use an enamel or glass container for the liquid, and one that is broad and shallow. Place the decorated articles in the bath, design side up, and allow to remain until the design stands about $1/8''$ in relief. Wash the pieces in cold water. The black paint is removed by soaking a short time

29

in turpentine and then rubbing the surface with a rag dipped in turpentine and pumice.

Polish the surface by rubbing with fine steel wool, and rub on some jeweler's rouge if you want a highly polished finish.

How to Make a Design

On paper, draw several outlines the same size as the piece you are planning to etch. Using black water color and a $\frac{1}{16}''$ brush, make a different design on each to see how it will appear on the finished product. At first, try to keep a $\frac{1}{4}''$ border around the metal and avoid lines of less than $\frac{1}{16}''$ in width. Broader areas make the etching easier to do. Figures 1, 2, and 3 show suggested designs, but try to make your own.

A round copper ash tray is one of the easiest projects because it can be etched without additional containers for the etching fluid. After the design is transferred to the tray and the parts covered with the acid resistant, the etching fluid may be poured into the depression as soon as the resistant is dry.

To make the ash tray, cut a disk 5" in diameter from 16 gauge sheet copper. The depression is made on a wooden mold or a sandbag. The mold is easier. Center the disk on the mold and pound it into shape with a rawhide hammer. This hammer will not scar the metal. When the tray is shaped, clean it with dampened pumice or very fine steel wool. Be sure that it is clean; otherwise, the acid resistant will not adhere during the etching.

The design is transferred to the metal with carbon paper placed face down on the metal and the design face up on the carbon paper. Trace the design with a hard pencil, being sure that the paper does not slip. With a $\frac{1}{16}''$ brush paint the design with the acid resistant. Paint the edge of the tray with a $\frac{1}{4}''$ border. Allow three or four hours for the paint to dry. Another method is to cover the entire face of the tray with melted paraffin after it is cleaned. Trace the design on the paraffin and scrape the design clean. This is not as accurate as the asphaltum but it uses the same method.

When the paint is dry, pour the acid mixture into the depression of the tray and the etching begins. When the exposed surface is $\frac{1}{32}''$ deep, the etching is completed. Follow earlier instructions for preparing the fluid and for cleaning and polishing.

A Silver, Nickel, or Copper Bracelet. Cut a piece of metal 6" long and 1" wide. Smooth the edges with steel wool and pumice. Plan the design on paper and transfer it to the metal with carbon paper. Figures 4 and 5 show suggested designs. Cover the design and border

ETCHING ON METAL

HOW TO MAKE A DESIGN

FIG. 1   FIG. 2   FIG. 3

ASH TRAY IN MOLD

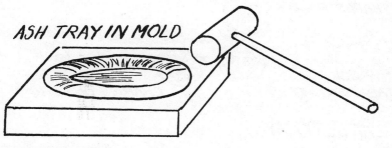

BRACELET

FIG. 4   FIG. 5

ETCHING BRACELET

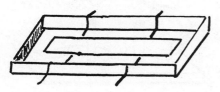

FIG. 6

SHAPING

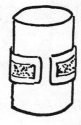

ETCHING ON METAL

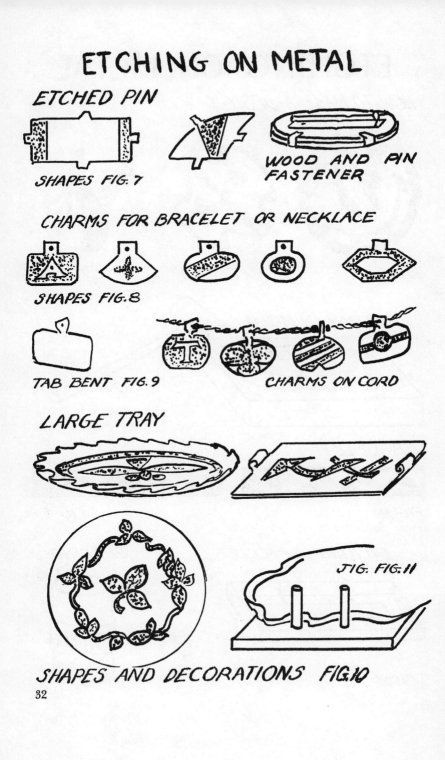

ETCHED PIN

SHAPES FIG. 7

WOOD AND PIN FASTENER

CHARMS FOR BRACELET OR NECKLACE

SHAPES FIG. 8

TAB BENT FIG. 9

CHARMS ON CORD

LARGE TRAY

SHAPES AND DECORATIONS FIG. 10

JIG. FIG. 11

with acid resistant. Also, cover the back and edges of the bracelet, since it is to be immersed in the etching fluid. Use a glass tray. When the resistant is dry, put the bracelet in the etching fluid. Two strings placed horizontally under the bracelet permit it to be lifted from the fluid to dispel the air bubbles which form (Fig. 6). This makes the etching smoother.

When the etching is deep enough, remove the bracelet from the fluid and wash it in clear water. Follow instructions for cleaning. Shape the bracelet around a mandrel or an oval stick.

An Etched Pin. Cut a piece of 16 gauge copper or nickel silver metal of the desired shape and smooth the edges. In planning the design include four points which are to hold a piece of wood to which the clasp is attached. Figure 7 shows suggested shapes. Plan the decorative design and transfer it to the metal. When the etching is completed, cut a piece of wood 1/8″ thick into the same shape as the front of the pin. Turn the points over it to hold it in place. Attach a pin back to the wood.

Etched Charms for a Bracelet or Necklace. A jeweler's saw and fine jeweler's saw blades are desirable for cutting the 16 gauge metal into the desired shapes. In planning the charms make an extra tab at the top for attaching to a cord or chain. Figure 8 shows suggested shapes and decorative designs. When the design has been etched, bore a small hole in each tab and with a pair of pliers bend it so it is at a 90° angle to the charm (Fig. 9). To string a charm on a cord, put a knot in the cord on each side of the charm to hold it in place. To string the charms on a chain, make a link of wire.

A Large Etched Tray. Copper in 16 or 18 gauge is a suitable metal for a tray. Cut a circular or oval shape the desired size. A piece 18″ in diameter makes a serviceable round tray. Plan a design for the center, leaving a 3″ margin which is plain. Transfer the design and paint all of the tray excepting the design with acid resistant. If the whole tray is to be immersed in etching fluid, be sure to paint the back, too. To avoid having to obtain as large a dish as this would require, turn up the edges of the tray before painting the design. The edges are turned with a jig (Fig. 11). Figure 10 shows suggested shapes and decorative designs.

Metal Foil Tooling

Tooled designs are made on very thin metal—30 to 36 in gauge. Copper, brass, or silver color can be used. The idea is to raise up designs in relief by pushing down the background.

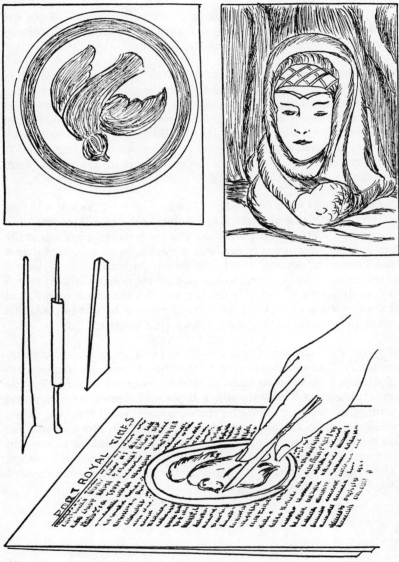

First, decide on the size of the article you wish to make. Use paper for a pattern. Now sketch on the design you want to transfer to the metal. Keep in mind that you must tool around the outline, so avoid small areas and lines. As a guide while work is proceeding, darken all portions that are to be raised.

Before transferring the design, you will want to prepare a padded area on the table on which to lay the metal. Use several layers of newspapers or thick cloth for this purpose. Now lay the piece of metal on the pad and place the design over it. Trace around the design with a pencil or sharp pointed instrument, press down a bit, and then remove the paper. Retrace the lines with the sharp end of a modeling tool to make them as deep as possible.

You are now ready to tool around the design. A leather modeler with tracer on one end and spoon on the other is commonly used for this purpose. However, you may make your own modeling tools from wooden dowels. Look at the illustration for suggested shapes. An orange stick may also be used.

Begin the modeling by pressing close to the edge of the design and moving the tool away toward the outer edge. Press down as much as possible, and move the tool back and forth over the back with smaller even strokes. After the design is raised on the front, turn the metal over and tool in reverse. This time push down on the design. Continue tooling first on one side and then on the other until design stands at least ¼" in relief.

After the background is lowered the design must be sculptured. In other words, if you are modeling a head, you must sculpture in hair, eyes, and other features on the raised design. This work must be done carefully and with less pressure applied to the tool.

After the article is completed, rub it carefully with steel wool. If you want to darken the tone of the metal, wash it with liver of sulphur. Dissolve a few crystals in some hot water and then apply to the metal with a soft rag. If the solution is too strong, the metal will become very dark. Wash first in water, then rub with steel wool and pumice until the metal becomes the proper tone.

If a bright polish is desired, any liquid metal polish can be used. A special paint may be purchased for adding color to the metal. This should be applied very skillfully; otherwise, it will cheapen the appearance of the picture.

PLASTICS

Plastic is an exciting medium that has gained in popularity because of its beautiful glasslike quality and its flexibility for molding into various forms. Plastic articles are appropriate in rooms with

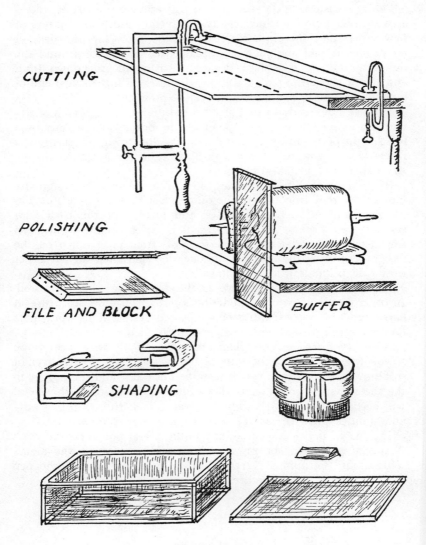

CUTTING

POLISHING

FILE AND BLOCK

BUFFER

SHAPING

ASSEMBLY

modern furniture and have become important in the decoration of this style home.

It is now possible to purchase plastics in almost any locality. They come in sheets 1/8" to 1" in thickness and in almost any color. Plastics are used so extensively in all fields of manufacturing that it is possible to buy them in a variety of shapes. For instance, rods, which come in all sizes, are sometimes grooved into interesting shapes, hollow tubes, and large solid blocks. If you live in a manufacturing city, visit some of the factories and pick up some scrap plastic which can be purchased for very little money.

Plastics are soft in comparison with metal and the surface is easily scratched. It is necessary to cover both sides with paper, even while you are working with it. Make a paper pattern of the article you wish to make, cut it out and fit the pieces together. If all the pieces are exact, trace the outline on the paper covering of the plastic. Cut around the outline with a coping saw; for fine work, use a jeweler's saw. You must devise a way to hold the work in place on a table while cutting and consider whether a vise will mar the plastic.

The next problem is to smooth the edges. This is done with a flat file. A triangular file is used for grooves or corners. Next, polish the edges on a buffing machine or use jeweler's rouge. If rouge is to be applied by hand, cut a piece of wood 1" by 3" by 6" and cover it with canvas or sturdy cloth. Put some rouge on the top and you have a buffing block.

After the pieces are cut and edges polished, they must be shaped before they are assembled. This is done by heating until the plastic becomes pliable and fits around a mold. It is possible to do this by boiling in water four or five minutes, but we suggest a regular heating oven for large pieces. Have your forms ready before removing the plastic from the heat, as it hardens in a few seconds. It is possible to re-heat the pieces if you are not successful at first.

Assemble your pieces and cement them in place with a plastic cement. Use Duco cement for some plastics and acetate for others, according to the type plastic you use.

A special dye may be purchased to add color to your article—also a special paint. Etched designs are especially attractive on plastics. Scratch on an outline of your design, then scrape it back and forth with a razor blade or sharp knife.

POTTERY

FIG.1

FIG.2   FIG.3

MUG

POTTERY

Pottery has universal appeal for children, teen-agers, men and women. It is perhaps the most creative of all crafts—if molds are avoided so that the worker may express his own personality. Blind persons are most successful at working with clay because of their sensitive fingers and awareness of contour and detail.

Before beginning this craft, you should know something about clay. It comes in all textures, from highly refined clay to coarser grades. It also comes in a wide range of colors including red, white, cream, black, and all shades of gray or brown. Therefore, if you find a clay bank near a stream, don't discard the idea of using the clay because of the color. In the first section of this book, we have told you how to prepare natural clay for use if it is suitable for pottery.

There are many methods of working clay, such as use of coils, slab, slip, and the potter's wheel. Because of lack of space, only the methods most commonly used by a beginner will be described.

The first step is to prepare the clay for modeling, which means that it must be the right consistency in regard to plasticity and texture. The clay must contain enough moisture to knead in the hand without sticking. It will fall apart if it is too dry. We suggest you make a wedging board for removing the air pockets.

A *wedging board* is a hard surface on which clay is cut in half and thrown one piece over the other with force. The operation is repeated until all air pockets and cracks are eliminated. Wedging is very important because most breakages in kilns are caused by air pockets left in the clay. A large plaster of Paris slab makes the best wedging board. Because of its porous quality, the extra moisture can be absorbed from the clay as it is thrown, or by wetting the slab more moisture can be added to give the clay the proper consistency. To make the wedging board, build a wooden frame about 22″ by 18″ and pour in the plaster of Paris to a depth of about 3″. Line the bottom of the frame with sand for a stronger foundation. Put a wooden slab at the back of the frame and stretch a taut wire diagonally from the top of it to the center of the frame. Piano wire is recommended. To mix plaster of Paris, sift the plaster into water until the water is filled up and a mound appears; then stir the mixture until creamy. Plaster should become quite warm, after which it cools and sets.

Coil Method. This method was used by the American Indians and is commonly used for making bowls and vases when a potter's wheel

39

is not used. To begin an article which is built of coils, cut a base the size and shape you wish to make. Then build up the sides with layers of rolled coils. You must have a flat, even surface for rolling the coils and it must be covered with a material that will not stick to the clay. Linoleum or oilcloth can be used for this purpose.

To make the coils, place a piece of clay on the table and roll it back and forth by using the palms of both hands (Fig. 1). Watch the thickness of the coil and roll it so that the diameter is the same throughout. The finished coil should be a little longer than the circumference of base to which it is to be attached. Place your base on a piece of heavy cardboard so it can be moved without breaking, and set it in front of you for attaching coils. Make slight impressions around rim of base with handle of brush and cover generously with slip. Now set your coil in place, cut ends to fit, and seal with more slip. Force the coil down firmly on the base and remove contours on both sides by pressing the clay down on the base (Fig. 2). Smooth the sides with your fingers or a modeling tool. Continue adding coils in this manner. If there is a flare in the wall, set the coils on the outer edge of previous coil; or if the wall is pulled in, reverse the procedure (Fig. 3). In order to do the shaping accurately you must make a profile of your article. This is called a template. (See illustration.) You can use this as a guide and keep the curves equal on all sides.

Slab Method. This method is used for making articles with flat bottoms. Make a cardboard pattern of your project according to pieces required. Roll the clay flat with the rolling pin and cut out the individual pieces. Care must be taken to roll the clay in equal thickness throughout (Fig. 4). This method is used for making small boxes, book ends, or tiles. The pieces are joined by making tiny depressions around the edges to be sealed. Cover with a generous amount of slip and force the edges together. Be sure all air pockets are removed before the edges are sealed.

Sculpturing Clay

A popular use of clay is the modeling of small figures. The figures must be sturdy enough to stand without an armature, and append-ages should be placed close to the body. Do not attempt to mold objects around a wire or wooden armature, as they cannot be fired. Begin with the amount of clay required for the figure you wish to make. Place it on a table covered with oilcloth and model it into general proportions. If the figure is thick, hollow out the center at this point so the clay will dry more readily. Use a modeling tool or

40

orange stick for modeling the features. If small pieces of clay must be added, groove the surface, cover well with slip, and force the new piece in place. Animals should be in a sitting or recumbent position in order to avoid appendages which do not fit close to the body (Fig. 5). In sculpturing figures, place the feet close together and arms next to the body (Fig. 6).

Slip. This is clay dissolved in enough water to make it the consistency of thick cream. Slip is used for joining pieces of clay together, attaching handles, and for duplicating objects.

Decorating. After shaping, the surface of the clay object can be decorated by: incising, which is producing line designs; carving, which is cutting away parts of the surface; modeling, which is adding clay motifs to the surface to produce a low relief. The clay object can also be painted in a slip or engobe, either as an all-over decoration, or by painting and then scratching through with a tool to expose the original color of the clay in various places. This method is called Sgraffito.

How to Fire Clay

Clay must be fired twice if glaze is to be added. The first firing is called biscuit; it is done with the same degree of heat that is

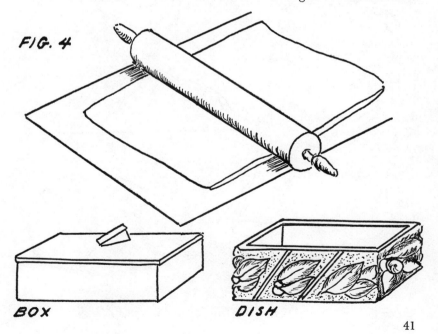

FIG. 4

BOX   DISH

POTTERY

CHRISTMAS FIGURES

FIG. 6

FIG. 5

required for glazes. The articles must be perfectly dry before they are placed in a kiln. This is of primary importance; otherwise, they will explode. Also, the drying should take place where there is a circulation of air; therefore the objects should not be shut in a cupboard.

Biscuit Firing. After the articles are dry, place them in a kiln to be fired. They may be stacked carefully near each other and on top of each other for the initial firing. Biscuit is fired very slowly. Each kiln has its own firing time. The usual temperature for biscuit is about 1850° F. After the kiln is turned off, the door must not be opened until the kiln has cooled. If it is opened before it cools, the pieces may crack or warp. As biscuit ware, the object can be painted in underglaze colors which are mixed with water and applied with brushes. The object is then covered with a transparent glaze and given a second firing. Transparent glaze can also be used over slip or engobe decoration.

How to Glaze

There are many types of glazes on the market in addition to transparent: majolica which is heavy and shiny, mat for a flat finish, and others. All must be fired according to the directions available. Glaze comes in powder form and must be mixed with water to the consistency of cream. Glazes of the same nature can be mixed for a great variety of colors. Biscuit is moistened with a damp sponge before glaze is applied. Glazes can be poured over the piece, painted on with a brush, or sprayed. Small pieces are sometimes dipped in the glaze.

When the glaze is thoroughly dry, the articles may be fired. They must be placed in the firing chamber without setting them directly on the shelf; otherwise, the glaze will stick the pottery to the shelf when it is cold. We do not recommend applying glaze to the base of an article, since it will drop on the kiln floor and harden. Later it has to be chipped off. Set the articles on stilts that can be purchased with the kiln or use small flat squares of fired biscuit which you can make yourself. You are now ready to close the kiln and begin the firing. Glazes are not fired as slowly as biscuit. They are prepared for use at specific temperatures and it is important to know firing time for particular glazes before they are placed in the kiln. Generally firing time for glazes is about 1800° to 1850° F. Do not open the door until the kiln is cool. If a glaze is not satisfactory, more glaze can be added and the article re-fired.

PAINTED TIN

WASTE BASKET
FROM AN OIL CAN

CANDLE HOLDER
FROM CAKE PAN

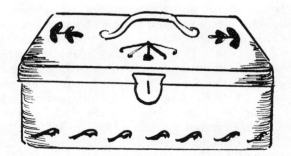

CANDLE HOLDER
MADE INTO A CHEST

44

TIN

Tin for the home craftsman is easily obtainable. The great variety of tin cans, in which coffee, fats, crackers, and canned goods come, can be used as they are, adding paint and decorations. Rectangular oil containers from garages come in larger sizes. These too are used as they are or are cut with tin snips to provide pieces for original design. When a large piece of tin is required, it is bought at a tinner's shop.

The equipment needed is a pair of tin shears, preferably with curved blades, steel wool for smoothing edges, and pliers for shaping and bending the metal. For more elaborate pieces a wooden mold, hammers, stamping tools, rivets, and soldering equipment will be needed.

Tin, unlike most of the other metals, is appropriately protected and beautified by paint, since its surface is subject to rust. Bare tin has a certain beauty and is used in Mexican crafts. Americans first knew the metal as it came from England with its japanned or lacquered finish, and have continued the custom as the traditional decoration for tin. Quick-drying enamel or lacquer is usually applied as a base coat, with the decoration added when the first coat is dry. Experience teaches that a quick-drying solvent should be used with oil paint which comes in tubes.

Early American crafts contribute an easy and practical way to decorate tin. The utensil was first painted a solid color. When it was dry, motifs were cut from wall paper and glued to the surface in any desired arrangement. Another way, of more recent origin, is to cut the designs from colored advertisements. You need not stick to tradition; create your own motifs and paint them on with oil paint or enamel.

If the surfaces are badly rusted, the rust can be removed with steel wool and kerosene before painting. Radiator paint is often used for the first coat. Examples of objects to decorate are candle molds, coffee pots, and tin boxes.

GOLD LEAF ON TIN AND WOOD

Frequent requests for ways to use gold leaf lead us to believe that the following directions for laying gold leaf on tin and wood will be useful:

1. Clean the surface and apply a priming coat. Let it dry.
2. Apply a coat of flat paint and let it dry.
3. Have the design on tracing paper. Rub the back of it with lithopone, which is a white pigment containing zinc sulphide. Lay it face up on the article. Secure it with scotch tape and trace the design with a hard pencil. Remove tracing paper.
4. With a small brush, paint gold size over the parts of the design on which gold leaf is to be laid. Gold leaf is bought in books at an art supply store. The size is purchased at the same place. Let the size dry until it is very tacky—sticky enough to pull when touched.
5. Lay a sheet of gold leaf face down over the sized surface and carefully press it with a pad of lintless cloth. Lift the sheet of gold leaf and cover any section of sized area which remains. Repeat this until all areas are covered with gold.
6. If any lines or details such as veins or flower centers are needed, etch them in a day later. Use a needle or other sharp instrument.
7. To tint gold leaf, use varnish colored with oil paint and a few drops of linseed oil. Paint it over the gold leaf a day after it has been laid. Be sure to paint it on neatly with a small brush. Let it dry.
8. If the object has no other decoration than the gold leaf, cover the surface with quick-drying clear varnish. Use three or four coats, rubbing each one but the last with very fine steel wool as they dry. Rub the last coat with a paste made of fine pumice and water.

A DECORATED TRAY

Prepare a tray, after it is cleaned well, with a coat of primer and two coats of flat black paint, being sure that each is dry before applying the next.

Draw the design on tracing paper, rub the back with lithopone, and transfer the pattern to the tray with a hard pencil.

The tray in the illustration is only a suggestion. You may secure a traditional pattern and copy it or design one of your own. Parts of it may be gold leaf, with the details etched or tinted with colored varnish. Shading is indicated with darker colors. The designs may be outlined with gold leaf or oil paint. Be sure to allow each coat to dry before superimposing another. When the painting is completed and dry, glaze the tray with several coats of varnish. The directions on the opposite page all apply to a tray.

TRAY WITH GOLD LEAF

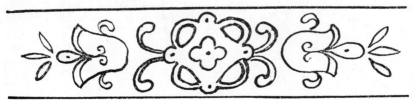

ANTIQUE CHAIRS

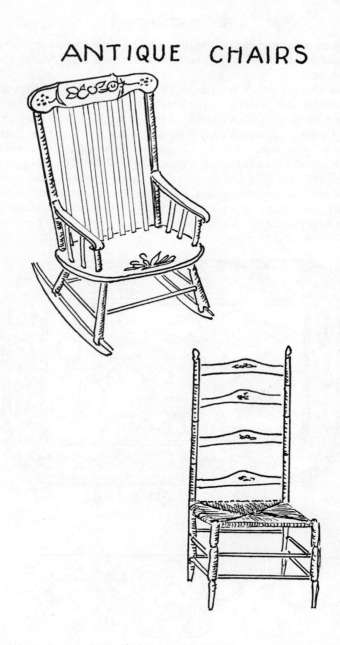

REFINISHING ANTIQUE FURNITURE

The process of removing old varnish or paint from antique articles is long and tedious. It must be done in such a way as not to discolor or mar the surface of the wood. Begin by soaking the surface well with varnish remover, and remove the old coating as it becomes soft and free from the wood. Work on a small area at a time and soak the carved surface again with varnish remover. Fold a piece of sandpaper over a thin piece of wood and use it to remove varnish in the depressed areas. After the varnish or paint is removed, repair any broken parts of the frame. Try to avoid using nails for joining new parts. The proper procedure is to drill holes in the two parts to be joined and fasten them together with wooden pegs. Cover the pegs with glue to secure them in place. For attaching flat pieces such as drawers, cut dovetail edges.

After the varnish is removed, the wood should be made perfectly smooth. Fill all cracks with plastic wood—if possible, make your own filler by mixing sawdust and glue. Remove the scratches with different grades of sandpaper or fine steel wool. Add stain and varnish as described on page 22. See "Caning a Chair Seat" (page 259) for adding a new seat.

Ladder-Back Chair. Prepare the surface by removing all the old varnish, as described above. Smooth the surface with sandpaper or steel wool. It is customary to rub the wood of this type chair with linseed oil before adding varnish. You might add a little burnt umber and burnt sienna oil paint to the oil to give it a warm, rich color. When this is dry, add one or two coats of clear hard varnish. Rub down with fine sandpaper and pumice powder. Now give it several coats of wax.

Painted Furniture. Some old pieces of furniture, such as Boston rockers or Hitchcock chairs, were painted black. On close inspection, you will see they are not a dead black, but have a reddish glow. This was done by giving the chair a coat of red paint first. A second coat of black paint was then added and allowed to dry. It was then rubbed down to a degree that the red glow of the first coat could appear. If you want to do an excellent job and feel equal to the rubbing, add a second coat of black paint.

Black chairs were usually decorated with stencil designs. For directions on how to apply gold leaf and oil paints, see page 46.

NEW FURNITURE FROM OLD

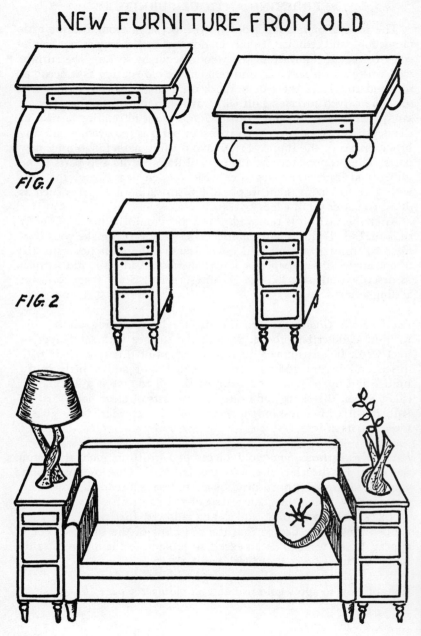

FIG. 1

FIG. 2

NEW FURNITURE FROM OLD

If you have an old piece of furniture which is out of style or too large for use, don't discard it until you consider the possibility of remodeling it. Almost any article that is made of good wood can be fashioned into a useful piece of furniture. This will require some imagination on your part, a saw, hammer, nails, and paint, plus some pleasant labor.

Coffee Tables. We have seen numerous types and sizes of old tables cut down and made into coffee tables for use in a living room. Library tables are excellent for this purpose because of size and shape. Old "marble top" tables also are popular. The marble top cannot be marred with liquids or scratches. Stands with a pedestal for the base present an easy problem and a round low table is quite pleasing. Even a round dining table can be cut down for use in a large room. Add a piece of plate glass or mirror as a covering for wooden tops.

End Tables. If you have a flat top desk not in use, why not cut away the center and use the ends for small chests to place beside a couch or bed. The drawers will be useful and you will have a place to set a lamp.

Remodeled Cupboards. Cupboards can have their faces lifted in many ways. If you have china and knickknacks to display, remove the doors. You can make a scalloped wooden frame for the edge to resemble a Dutch cupboard. A cheap modern secretary was transformed into a beautiful piece of furniture. It was painted white and antiqued with burnt umber, then finished with a coat of clear lacquer. The glass in the bookcase was painted in Chinese designs.

Dressing Table. An old table or stand is used for a base. Add a ruffle in a material to match your room. Cover the top with the same material, or a lace mat if you have one the correct size. Protect the top with a piece of plate glass. An old picture frame can be used for the covering if it is the same size as your table top.

One of the greatest problems in making over old furniture is the refinishing of the wood. The old varnish should be removed whether it is to be painted or finished in the natural wood. The outer coat can be removed with varnish remover, but it will take some hand work to remove stains from cracks and crevices. If you want to bleach the wood to a lighter color, cover it with a paste made with flour and household lye. Clorox can also be used in the paste in place of lye. Elsewhere in this book we have described how to add paint to finish wood in its natural color. (See page 22.)

SPATTER PRINTING

Spatter printing is done by cutting a design from a piece of heavy paper and placing it on the material you wish to decorate. Pin the design securely in place and spatter the background with a paint or dye in a contrasting color. When the cutout is removed, you will have a silhouette of the design the color of the original material.

How to Make Spatter Prints. Cover a table with several layers of newspaper—you need extra thickness for pinning designs in place. Place the material on the table, then arrange design over the top and secure in place with pins around the edges, as shown below. Now spatter the background by spraying with a spray gun, which can be purchased at any hardware store.

The type of spray you use depends on the article you wish to spatter print. If you have a background of paper, ordinary poster paint is used. The paint must be thinned by adding the same amount of water. A concentrated dye is suitable for cloth—so the material can be washed. Enamel paint thinned somewhat with turpentine is used for spraying posters or rugs.

Suggested Projects for Spatter Prints

Greeting Cards (Fig. 1). Children need only go to the woods or yard to find motifs for their designs. Leaves, flowers, ferns, or grasses make beautiful prints if the arrangement is correct. Colored construction paper is generally used for the background and poster paint selected for the spray. If you are planning to make a number of cards, or working with a group, buy a package of paper in assorted colors and

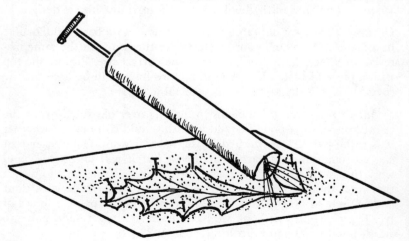

SPATTER PRINTING

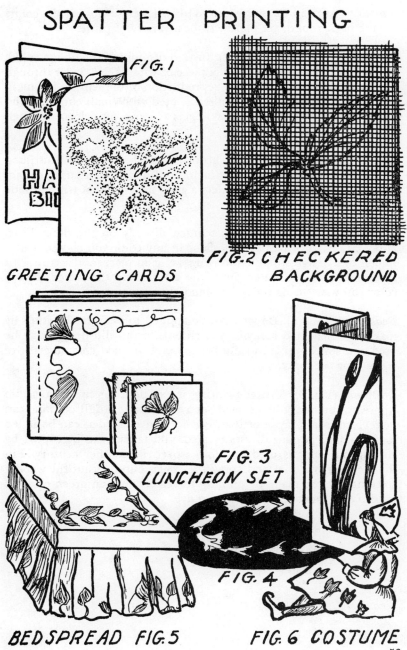

FIG. 1

GREETING CARDS

FIG. 2 CHECKERED
BACKGROUND

FIG. 3
LUNCHEON SET

FIG. 4

BEDSPREAD FIG. 5

FIG. 6 COSTUME

use white paint in the spray gun. This will save changing the colors for the background, yet there will be a variety of prints.

Checkered Background (Fig. 2). Instead of pinning the design to the printing material, cover it with a piece of wire screen. Spray through the screen and you will have a reproduction of the wire in the mesh as well as the design. This method is used with small children who lack sufficient strength in their fingers to push pins down through the paper.

Luncheon Sets. Beautiful luncheon sets can be made, as illustrated in Figure 3. Materials such as linen, muslin, organdy, and gingham are most suitable. Be sure to select a good material that will not fade when washed.

Rug. The rug in Figure 4 is painted directly on the floor. First, apply two coats of paint to the floor in any color you choose. Cut a stencil in a design suitable for a rug, lay it in place, and secure with a paste of flour and water. Spray the cutouts and the stencils in any color you wish, using the same brand of paint as on the floor.

Bedspreads (Fig. 5). Designs can be applied to bedspreads either by making stencils and spraying the cutouts, or a solid design may be used and spray applied to the background. A good commercial dye is used for the spray.

Costumes (Fig. 6). Spatter printing is excellent for use in a studio where costumes are being made or re-modeled. A dull costume can be revived by a spray of brilliantly colored dye. Borders can be added to skirts, and peasant dresses created. Old fabrics can be copied by cutting out designs used on cloth woven in another century. Pin them to the material and spray the background. Beautiful woodsy costumes can be made by pinning leaves or vines on green cambric muslin and spraying with a brown dye.

TIE DYEING

Tie dyeing has a quality of magic in it because the patterns are ever varying and as the colors run together the most unusual effects are created. That does not mean that you have no control over this craft. Here are three ways of placing the centers of interest in the patterns. All of these are effected by the folding of the cloth and the way strings are tied around the cloth to hold it in place during the dyeing.

The first and simplest is to fold the material into four layers and wrap string around it tightly. There are white lines on the cloth where the string crosses. Each end of the bundle may be dipped in different colors. (See illustration A.) To get a center pattern, wad a piece of cloth into a ball and tie as shown in Figure B. Figure C shows a way to have corner motifs. Your own ingenuity can devise other plans of tying.

For best results in dyeing, wet the bundles in clean warm water and while wet, dip them in any commercial dye. Follow the directions for regular dyeing as they are given on the package.

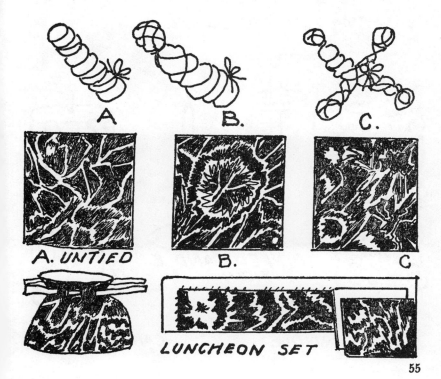

A.   B.   C.

A. UNTIED   B.   C

LUNCHEON SET

CANDLES

COOKIE CUTTER MOLDS   FIG. 1

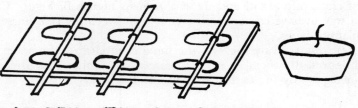

MUFFIN TIN MOLDS FIG. 2

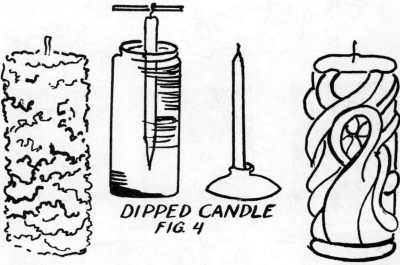

DIPPED CANDLE
FIG. 4

FIG. 3
FLUFFY CANDLE

FIG. 5
CARVED CANDLE

CANDLES

Candles are fun for children to make because of the fascination of this tiny light. It belongs to Christmas and has lighted homes of all ages. Candle making is also a practical craft, as the many candle ends that accumulate can be re-melted and made into beautiful candles.

During Colonial days candles were made from tallow rendered from beef and mutton. Later, beeswax was added to make them burn slower. Today, candles are usually made from paraffin. For making at home, candle ends may be used. If you want a candle in a pure light color, use paraffin and then color it by adding wax crayons. The molds used may be either baking equipment or tin cans.

Cookie Cutter Molds (Fig. 1). It is easy to find cookie cutters in the shape of stars and any number of interesting shapes. Cut a base of heavy cardboard and punch a hole in the center for a wick. Cut a small stick to lay across the top and run a string which is tied to the stick down through the hole in the base. Tie a knot in the end of the string to keep it tight. Since the base is made of cardboard, pour in a little wax at first and allow it to partly harden before filling the mold. Set the mold in hot water a few seconds before removing the candle.

Muffin Tin Molds (Fig. 2). If you want to make a number of candles at one time, use old muffin tins.

Fluffy Candles (Fig. 3). A large candle is best for this. Use a large can for the mold. Punch a small hole in the center of the bottom. Use a small stick across the top of the can and tie a piece of candle wick or soft string to the stick. Run the string through the can and out the hole in the bottom. Knot it to keep it tight. This makes the wick. Set the mold in cold water and fill it with melted wax. When the candle is hard, it may need some additional wax to fill the can. To remove the candle, cut off the knot and cut the stick loose at the top. Set the mold in hot water for a short time and the candle can be slipped out. The coating is made by melting paraffin and beating it with an egg beater. Spread it on like cake icing. Cover the sides and top, being sure that the wick is not covered. Candles may also be dipped (Fig. 4).

Carved Candles (Fig. 5). Candles are excellent objects for carving. If you cannot find one the general size or shape you want, make a mold and pour your own. For carving in relief, you draw the pattern on the sides of the candle and cut away the wax to the depth desired, leaving the design raised. The design may be cut away to a depth of ⅛" to make a variation. Linoleum or wood carving tools are best but a knife of any kind may be used.

MOBILES

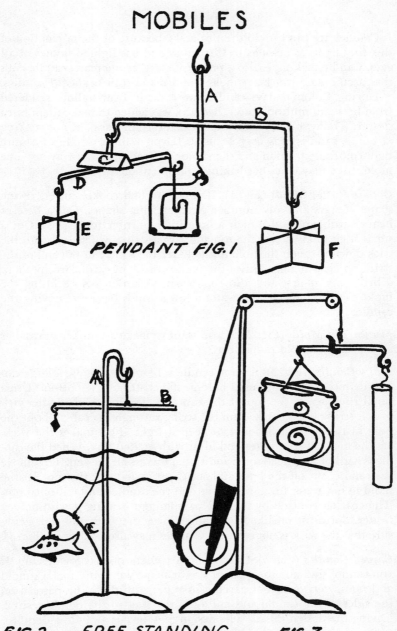

PENDANT FIG. I

FIG. 2   FREE STANDING   FIG. 3

58

MOBILES

Mechanics and art are joined to create these entertaining assemblies of metal, cord, wire, clay, or almost any material that is available. Some of them tell a story; others hold the observer's attention because of the ingenious ways by which they are balanced. Balance is maintained by the arrangement of the units of the design.

Figure 1 shows a pendant mobile. It is made of wire, a block of wood, and pieces of copper and aluminum foil. The piece A which is attached to the hook is a loop of fine wire. The heavier wire B has a hook in each end with about one third of it bent to form the lower hook. C is a polished block of wood with the wire D attached to the under side. A small wire loop attaches the upper side of the block to the hook above it. Wire D with a hook at each end balances intersecting pieces of plastic on one end E and a coiled wire at the other end. A cord is attached to the plastic with cement and tied to the hook above. The coil of wire for the other end of D is arranged to balance the plastic "fan." This is done by moving the wire D to the right place on the wooden block C. The "fan" F is made like E but is larger and is attached to the hook on B. Wire B with all units attached is balanced through the loop A. The hook at the top is screwed into a frame so the mobile hangs free.

The second mobile is free standing and shows a fish under the water with a baited hook and fishing rod balanced above. Plaster of Paris or clay forms a base for the heavy upright wire A. The rod B has a hook and bait at one end and fine wire twisted around the other end. It is balanced by a fine wire loop attached to the hook on A. The wires forming the waves are soldered to A. The fish is cut from light metal. Wire C, which holds the balanced fish, is soldered or bound to the upright A. A fine wire is attached to C and to A.

Figure 3 shows further possibilities of mobile construction. There is no limit to the number of units or the variety of their arrangement as long as they balance.

Little children will enjoy making mobiles with crayons and paper. One idea to try might be a circus. The trapeze performers can be suspended on short strings from the top of the window; animals hung from longer strings so they almost touch the window sill. The air currents in the room will set the whole thing in motion.

COPPER SCREEN

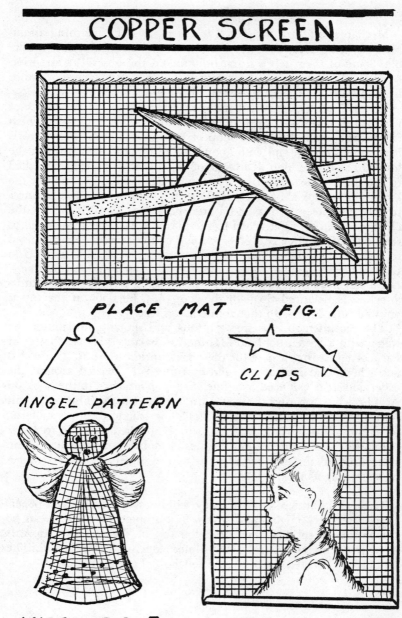

PLACE MAT   FIG. 1

CLIPS

ANGEL PATTERN

ANGEL FIG. 3   PORTRAIT   FIG. 2

COPPER SCREEN

Copper screen has a beauty which makes it a suitable background for some useful home decorations. Tin snips and pliers are the only necessary tools.

Place Mat (Fig. 1). Cut a piece of screen 15″ by 11″ for the base. Thirty gauge sheet copper is used for the decorations. Cut geometric or natural designs from the copper. At intervals on the design, leave small points for attaching to the screen. This is something to remember for all cutouts which will be attached to the screen. The design may be cut in units and interwoven; tapping with a nail gives a stippled effect for variety.

If a raised pattern is desired, tool the design before you cut it out. Fill the back with plastic wood.

For the binding at the outer edge of the mat, cut strips of light copper 1″ wide and fold. Turn the corners by folding the copper into a mitre without cutting it. Join strips, if necessary, at the corners by folding at a 45° angle. Use a wooden hammer to pound frame flat.

Portrait (Fig. 2). Trace a profile photograph using only the head and shoulders. Transfer it to soft copper. Draw the features and hair with a leather tool. If you wish to raise the cheeks, turn the copper over, lay it on a soft surface, and use a spoon to press the cheeks into a concave surface.

When all the tooling is completed, cut out the copper profile, and attach to the screen as instructed.

Cut a piece of screen as shown in the illustration. A piece of colored silk or paper and a piece of cardboard are cut the same size as the screen. Attach the profile to the screen by putting the points of copper through the mesh and pressing them flat. Lay the silk or paper over the clips, put the cardboard over this, and bend the edges with the copper strip as explained for the place mat.

Angel or Other Figure (Fig. 3). Cut a paper pattern as shown in the illustration. Cut the same shape from copper screen. Close the back of the body by sewing it with a fine wire which can be raveled from the screen. Cut the wings from light sheet copper or screen and attach at the back of the neck. The halo is made of a circle of the twisted wire and attached to the back of the head. Use blue beads for eyes. A red bead makes the mouth. Larger beads are used for the skirt. These are attached with the fine wire.

FOUR USEFUL BAGS

GRAPE DESIGN
BEADS FOR GRAPES
FELT FOR LEAVES
FIG. 1

CORN DESIGN
BEADS FOR CORN
FIG. 2.

CUT OUT DESIGN
FELT FOR FRUIT
FIG. 3

APPLIQUÉ
DESIGN
FIG. 4

FOUR USEFUL BAGS

Bags are essential to most women to carry knitting and sewing equipment or to take to the store when shopping. It is easy to make a bag in an original design, as the material can be salvaged from a rag bag and there are numerous ways of adding a decoration. Materials such as beads, felt, leather, or silk can be utilized. Here are directions for making four bags that may appeal to you.

Grape Design (Fig. 1). This bag is most attractive if made of monk's cloth or other loosely woven material. Cut the frame from wood; be sure to cut across the grain to make the handles stronger. Make a series of small holes about ¼" apart near the bottom of the frame. These are used for sewing the bag to the frame. Use large purple wooden beads for the grapes. Arrange them as shown. Green felt is most appropriate for leaves, but any green material may be used.

Corn Design (Fig. 2). Make a bag of burlap, monk's cloth, or other suitable material. The corn decoration is obtained by using pale yellow wooden beads and mercerized embroidery cotton. Place the beads in long even rows to resemble an ear of corn. Add long stitches of green embroidery thread around edges for corn silk. The long leaves may be made of a soft green material, or embroidered with long and short stitches.

Felt Designs (Fig. 3). Shopping bags are most attractive if decorated with designs cut from felt. The bag can be made of any sturdy material such as denim, sailcloth, or oilcloth. Draw a large picture of a fruit or vegetable. Transfer design to the felt and cut it out. Appliqué it to the front of the bag.

Appliqué Design (Fig. 4). This shopping bag is made of muslin or plain gingham. It is important to select a material easy to sew in order to appliqué a design. A lining may be added to make the bag more sturdy. If you are at loss for a design, copy one from an old quilt.

STENCILS

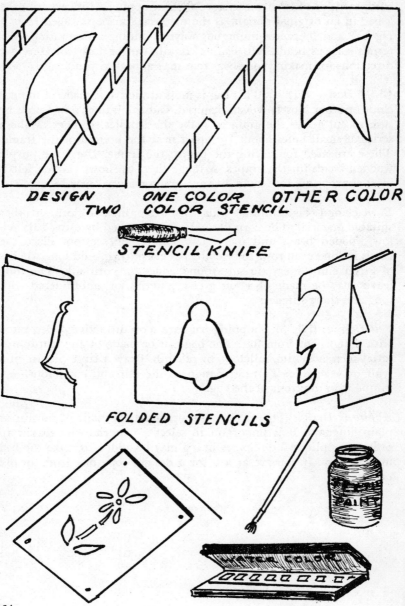

DESIGN   ONE COLOR   OTHER COLOR
TWO COLOR STENCIL

STENCIL KNIFE

FOLDED STENCILS

STENCILS

Stencils are among America's earliest forms of decoration. They are found on early furniture, walls, floors, and utensils. Stenciling is a method in which the design is drawn on heavy waxed paper or tin in such a way that all parts of the pattern can be cut out. The remaining part is the stencil. It is placed over the surface which is to be decorated and the paint is applied to the open parts of the stencil. A stiff, stubby brush is used. Several colors may be applied to the same stencil. If two areas of different color are adjacent, a piece of the stencil is used as a shield for the one while the other is being painted.

Bisymmetric patterns are easily made by folding lightweight stencil paper and cutting half of the design with scissors. When it is unfolded the stencil is ready.

A stencil is adapted to repetitive patterns, but if used only once it is an aid to inexperienced painters because it controls the edges of the pattern.

Wood, tin, cloth, and paper are suitable for stencil painting. For wood and tin, an oil-bound paint is usually best. Water-bound paints are used on paper, and textile paints give the best results on cloth. Directions for setting textile paints accompany the colors and should be followed closely.

Different strokes with the brush give varied effects. Some of the surface should show through the paint. Strokes are crossed sometimes, and stippled effects are secured by tapping the blunt end of the brush on the design. Color is used sparingly. A variety of colors results from painting one over another.

Stenciled designs on paper transform it into colorful decorations. Place mats for special occasions, personalized napkins, stationery, shelf paper, and place cards are a few of the possibilities. Opaque colors such as tempera give greater intensity, while transparent colors are more brilliant.

Furniture refinishers make use of stencils for both modern and antique pieces. For wooden and tin trays, plates, and boxes, this is a suitable decoration. Bare floors are made more interesting by using stencils on them. Borders and panels for walls are made from stencils.

Draperies, bedspreads, luncheon sets, and costumes can be made quite attractive with stencil paints.

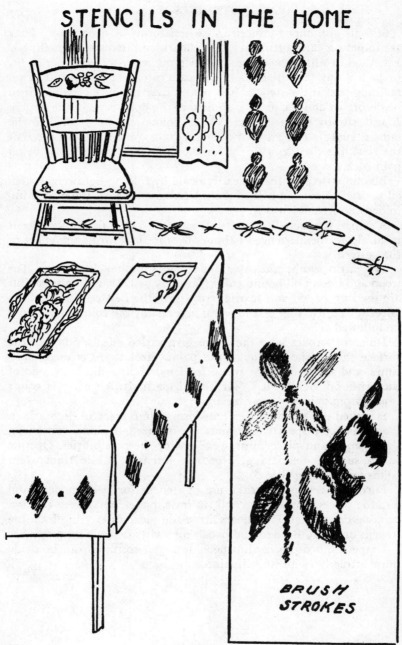

BRUSH
STROKES

DRIFTWOOD

Driftwood is wood that has remained in salt water for a long time and is finally washed up on the shore. Because of its long stay in the water, it is beaten by the waves and worn into interesting shapes. It is saturated with chemicals. The surface is very smooth and highly polished, so it needs no other finish. Because of its light gray color and unusual shapes, it can be made into many interesting projects. The illustration below may give you some ideas.

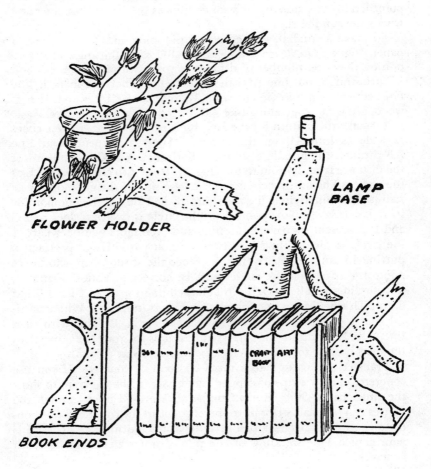

FLOWER HOLDER

LAMP BASE

BOOK ENDS

SUNDIAL

Many sundials are seen in yards, gardens, and public places but few people regard them as anything but a decoration. Although there are only four days in the year when the sundial and the clock can coincide—April 15, June 15, September 1, and December 24—sundials do tell fairly accurate time.

A sundial is made up of three parts: the gnomon, or stile, which casts the shadow; the face which bears the numerals; and the pedestal. The shape of the gnomon is a triangle with the angle at the point having the same number of degrees as the latitude of the place where the sundial stands.

To make a sundial, first construct the gnomon. Cut a square of paper (Fig. 1). On it, make a triangle ABC, with the angle at B containing the same number of degrees as your latitude. Lines CB and AB are straight but line AC can be curved or otherwise shaped. The finished gnomon may be cut from $\frac{1}{16}$" copper or $\frac{1}{2}$" wood. If it is wood, allow $\frac{1}{2}$" edge along line AB for fastening it to the face.

To make the pattern for the face, use a square of paper three times as wide as line AB on the gnomon. Draw a perpendicular line AB through the middle of it and a horizontal line CD one third of the distance from bottom to top (Fig. 2). Draw two circles, using E as the center. The outside circle has the long side of the gnomon for its radius. The inner circle has the short straight side of the gnomon for its radius (Fig. 3). Now point A on the circle is twelve o'clock and C and D represent six o'clock morning and evening. The upper part of the circle is divided first into twelve equal parts. Use a protractor, putting 15° in each space (Fig. 3). Since the shadows are shorter at noon, the spaces on the circle must be corrected. Follow Figure 4, putting lines parallel to AB through each point marked 1 2 3 4 5 and 6 on each side. Make lines parallel to CD as indicated. Where vertical line 1 crosses horizontal line 1, make an X. Do this with each line. The X's indicate the corrected positions for your time divisions, the ones nearest to twelve o'clock being narrowest (Fig. 5).

Transfer this pattern to a piece of wood or concrete. If you use concrete, narrow strips of copper may be set in the concrete to show the time spaces. Since Roman numerals are used on a sundial, the figures can be small strips of copper also set in the concrete. The concrete can be poured in a pan or other round form. The pedestal is your choice. One we know of is a pile of stones held together with concrete.

Some mottoes for sundials are "I count only the sunny hours," "Light rules me, The shadow thee," "None can call again the passed time," and "Make the passing shadow serve thy will."

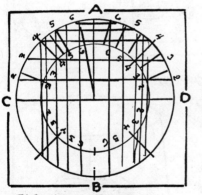

FIG. 1

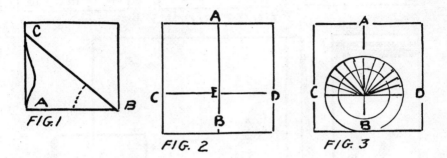

FIG. 2

FIG. 3

FIG. 4

FIG. 5

APPLIQUE

QUILT BLOCKS

DRAPERY

LUNCHEON SET

GUEST
TOWELS

DRESSING TABLE
FLOUNCE

APPLIQUÉ

Appliqué is the cutting out of designs from different colors of material and sewing them to a neutral background. This form of decoration is used on quilts, luncheon sets, curtains, aprons, and many other household accessories. Interesting motifs can also be cut from printed material and the individual pieces applied to other material with appliqué.

Cutting

The first problem in appliqué is to cut out a design. Make a paper pattern the exact size of design and then transfer it to a piece of cardboard. Now draw a line all the way around the outline ¼" beyond the edge. This will allow for enough material to turn in around the edges. Cut out the pattern and smooth the edges so it can be transferred evenly to the material. Lay the pattern on the cloth and trace around it with a pencil. Cut out the design with a pair of sharp scissors and if you have a number of cutouts that match, string them on a piece of thread. It is important to store them away perfectly flat to make the sewing easier when they are being applied.

Turning in Edges

The same amount of cloth must be turned in carefully on all edges. Turn in about ¼" as indicated on your pattern. Do the first turning in with the fingers and pinch in place. When you come to a curve or deep depression, make ⅛" snips in the cloth which will allow for the turn. The next step is to baste the edges down to keep them in place for sewing. Be sure to start with the end of thread on right side of cloth so it can be easily removed after the motif is applied.

Another method of turning in the edges is to cut the cardboard pattern the exact size of the design, fold the edges up over the cardboard, and press in place with a warm iron.

Sewing the Design

Assemble the pieces of your design, place them on the background cloth, and baste in place. If you are making squares for an appliquéd quilt, it is helpful to press diagonal lines radiating out from center of square to use as a guide for placing designs.

After the pieces are basted in place, you are ready to sew down the edges. Use a short, thin needle, and thread that matches colors in your design. The best stitch is what quilters have been calling a "blind stitch," because very little thread shows when the stitch is

71

completed. Bring the needle up through the foundation and both layers of design, then put it back in the foundation as near to this point as possible. Now carry the thread underneath for the stitch and bring the needle back up to the top. For an even edge, make the stitches as small as possible.

Appliqué can be used for decorating cotton, silk, thin woolens such as challis, or rayons. It is impossible to turn in coarse or thick material around the edges. However, designs cut from lightweight fabrics may be appliquéd on a heavy background.

You will find use for appliqué designs in decorating many household articles. It is an easy way to add bits of color, and your ragbag should supply the material you need. If you are not artist enough to draw your own designs, cut them from printed fabrics and apply them in the same manner. You can find pictures of flowers, leaves, butterflies, and other things, that can be assembled into a pleasing picture. We would like to suggest that luncheon mats or tablecloths made from organdy and decorated with appliqué are most successful. Use bits of colored organdy or handkerchief linen for the designs.

QUILTING

Quilting today has many more uses than holding a quilt together. When this old craft was brought over from Europe, it was used for making warm clothing and bedding to stave off the rigors of winter. A quilted cover is made up of three layers of materials—an inner layer of cotton with a covering on each side. Crisscross designs are stitched over the surface to hold the cotton in place. The criterion for fine quilting is a good design—usually geometric in nature—and small, even stitches.

The first step in quilting is to prepare the three layers for stitching. You can buy cotton especially prepared for quilting. It comes in a large sheet which is folded over several times and then rolled into a package. Be sure to unroll it very carefully and watch that none of the folds stick as they are taken apart. Any light woven material may be used for covering the two sides. The important point to remember in selecting a fabric is that it must be loosely woven so a needle can slip through easily. Muslin is a favorite lining for a quilt, but it should be tested for easy penetration of the needle.

Preparing Layers for Quilting

After the top layer is decorated, press carefully with an iron and be sure all edges are exactly straight. Next, cut the bottom layer and make the outside dimensions somewhat larger than the covering layer. If you are making a quilt, the bottom layer should extend several inches beyond the top, for the purpose of attaching to the quilting frame. Spread the layer to be used for lining out on the floor or a table. Unfold the cotton and lay on top, being sure that there are no lumps and all areas are of equal thickness. Baste the cotton into place with long stitches in diagonal lines leading from the center and then around the outside about ½" from the edges. Now lay on the top or decorated layer, fit the edges together, and baste into place. (See Figs. 1, 2, and 3.)

Quilting Patterns

Quilting patterns are usually such shapes as diamonds, triangles, or circles. However, the modern quilts often break this tradition by using flower forms or other motifs in their design. The usual rule is to plan a decorative design for important areas and then fill in the background with small diamonds or diagonal lines. Make a sketch of your design on paper, cut out all units that are repeated, and make a cardboard pattern. Note that a design such as "Feathers" required only one pattern that is repeated many times on either side of a cir-

QUILTING

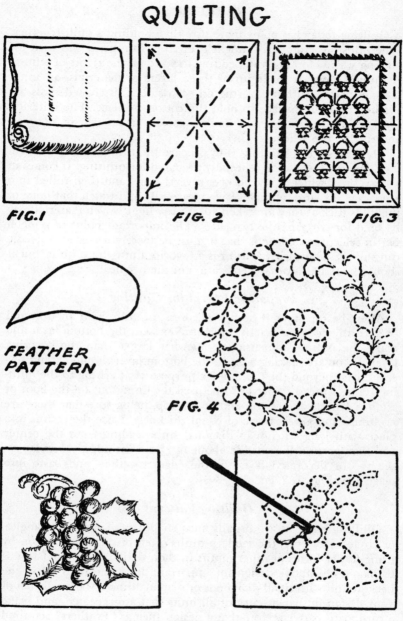

FIG.1

FIG. 2

FIG. 3

FEATHER
PATTERN

FIG. 4

FIG 5

74

cle (Fig. 4). To apply the design to cloth, trace lightly with a lead pencil and make narrow lines. It is a good idea to block out the quilting designs on the entire area before the sewing is started. You will then be sure all designs are the correct size and fit together perfectly.

Stitching. It is necessary to use a short, thin needle for making the stitches. Use a number 60 thread for quilting most cottons. Avoid threading your needle with a long thread; you will save time drawing it through the cloth. It also rubs thin from friction and may break. To begin sewing, tie a knot on the end of thread and gently force it through the first layer so it will be hidden from sight. Place your left hand underneath the padding to hold it firm and make two or three stitches with the needle. Draw the thread through and pull it tight. Continue sewing, making the stitches as small and even as possible.

It is most important that the three layers are held evenly in place while the stitching takes place. Large articles, such as quilts, are usually attached to a frame and the top and bottom are held taut throughout the quilting. However, it is possible to quilt small pieces without a frame. If you are using this method, quilt around the outside first so the edges will remain straight and even. Next, begin sewing in the center and out gradually to the border. It is possible to stitch individual squares for a quilt and set them together later, thus avoiding the use of a frame.

Raised Designs. It is possible to emphasize your designs by adding more cotton. This is done after the outline is stitched. Puncture the back of each unit with a crochet hook and force cotton in, a little at a time, until the area is packed evenly. It is not necessary to patch the hole as cotton will not come out if packed solidly. With this method you can use less cotton in the background, thus making the sewing easier (Fig. 5).

Binding Edges. There are two methods of binding edges. One is to trim the edges all around and bind with bias tape. The other is to trim the lower layer 1/4″ shorter than the one on top, also cutting away the cotton. Next, turn in the upper edge and bring back over the lower layer. Sew in place with blind stitches. Be sure all edges remain straight while stitching takes place, as binding is an important operation.

QUILTING

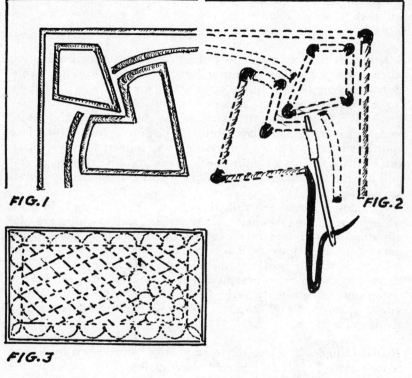

FIG. 1

FIG. 2

FIG. 3

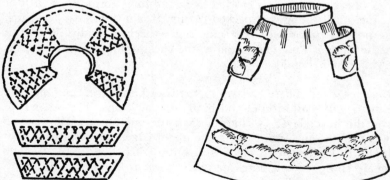

FIG. 4

FIG. 5

Corded Quilting

This method of quilting binds two pieces of cloth together and the middle layer of cotton is omitted. It also varies from the other type of quilting, since the design is transferred to the lower layer and the quilting done on the reverse side. The designs are raised by pulling a cord through parallel lines of stitches as shown in Figure 1.

Draw a design, then trace a second line about $\frac{1}{4}$" from the edge to allow for the cord. Trace it on the foundation layer, or foundation. Use a very loosely woven material that can be easily stitched. After the design is applied, lay the foundation on a table, design down, and cover with material you wish to use for the surface. Baste the two layers together thoroughly so they will stay in place.

Use a short, thin needle to do the stitching and try to match the color of thread with the top covering. When the stitching is completed, run a cord through the design. Use a very soft string such as candle wicking for the purpose. Thread the cord through a bodkin or blunt needle in order to force it through the channels. When you have completed a circle or reach a sharp turn, force the bodkin out of the cloth and then insert it again near the same point (Fig. 2).

For many years, quilting was employed only in making quilts. Today it is used as a decoration on table accessories (Fig. 3), cushion tops, pot holders, etc. It is most frequently used on such clothing as bed jackets, collar and cuff sets (Fig. 4), and even skirts are quilted (Fig. 5).

HOOKED RUGS

MODERN RUG

STAIR PAD   CHAIR SEAT

WELCOME MAT

HOOKED RUGS

Rug hooking is a popular folk craft. Such articles as chair seats, mats, stair pads, can be hooked. We know one woman who made a set of pads for her stairs, each one depicting a scene that was dear to her—a covered bridge, the little red schoolhouse, the dinner bell, flowers in the garden, and so on. Rugs can also be hooked in geometric designs to fit into a modern setting. If the design is made up of squares, you may hook one at a time on a small frame (Fig. 1). Then sew them together.

To hook a rug, make a frame of soft pine in the dimensions of the rug. Use a good quality of burlap for the foundation and tack to the frame. Almost any soft, strong material is suitable for hooking. An old wool blanket dyed in delicate colors is excellent, or nylon stockings, wool dresses, or even yarn may be used. Avoid silks or heavy worsteds. Cut the strips ½" to ¾" in width, according to weight of cloth.

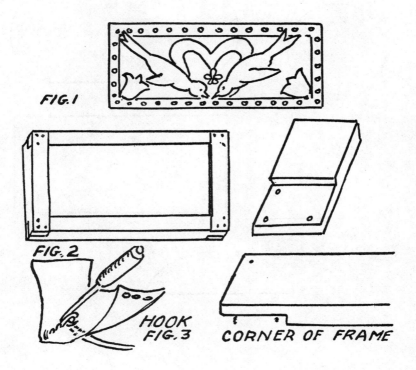

FIG. 1

FIG. 2

HOOK FIG. 3

CORNER OF FRAME

Trace design on top of burlap with colored crayons. Be sure you have enough rags in each color to carry out the planned design, as it is difficult to match shades for solid backgrounds. Secure a hook similar to the one in the illustration, and you are ready to work.

The hooking is done by holding the rag tight against the back with fingers of left hand and pulling it up through one of the holes in the burlap with hook in right hand. A loop is thus formed around the hook and must be pulled up about $\frac{1}{4}"$ or more, but each loop must be the same height. Always outline the design first and then fill in the centers. For even hooking, follow holes in burlap. Go into every hole if fine material is used for hooking; skip every other hole with heavier rugs. Continue until all holes are filled.

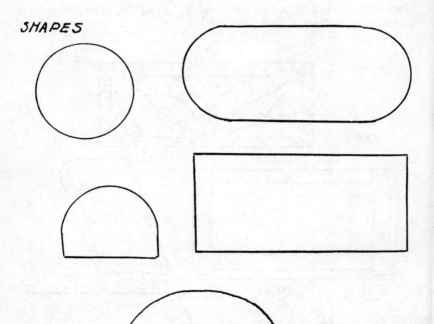

SHAPES

3

Crafts for Personal Adornment

From prehistoric times to the present day, people have made things to enhance their personal appearance. Their aim was not only to attract attention or beautify themselves, but to allay their superstitious fears. Present-day craftsmen smile at the latter but many of their products reflect its influence. The charms of the ancient people were their protection against evil, but today they are a way of adding interest to costumes.

Designers frequently turn to the jewelry of the early Egyptians and find it in keeping with modern living. Their fine workmanship and good design is ageless, and a challenge to any craftsman. The filigree jewelry of the ancient Chinese as well as the carving of precious stones has not been equalled even with modern mechanical equipment. It sets a standard toward which to strive. Most of us cannot become so skillful, but what we do can be in good taste and be functional in its construction.

Personal adornment is divided into utilitarian and ornamental uses. Nearly all of the things we make have both qualities. Appropriate material and design should be chosen because it must be remembered that hours of work are often involved and anything short of personal satisfaction will be a great disappointment.

The making of costume jewelry is one of the popular activities in a craftshop. It costs very little, as scrap materials can be utilized and metal findings are the only necessary purchases. Since jewelry is made from all mediums, why not start a box for odds and ends such as plastics, wood, felt, beads, metal, wire, and leather. Natural materials such as shells and seeds make beautiful necklaces that can be worn with sport clothes and sweaters. The seeds must be gathered in the fall, so spend a day in the country collecting material for the winter.

81

The making of articles for personal adornment can be profitable for the craftsman. Handmade jewelry and leather articles are most popular in gift shops. These articles can be made in a home workshop and can become an avocation if a person wants to do creative work aside from his regular job.

MINIMUM TOOLS FOR LEATHER WORK

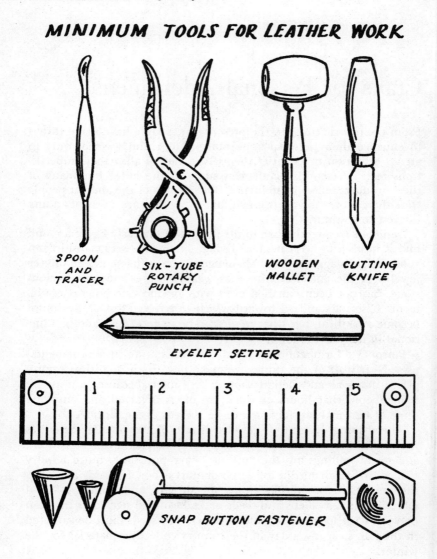

SPOON
AND
TRACER

SIX - TUBE
ROTARY
PUNCH

WOODEN
MALLET

CUTTING
KNIFE

EYELET SETTER

SNAP BUTTON FASTENER

LEATHERCRAFT

Before trying your skill in working with leather, you should know something about the medium itself. There are two types of leather—tooling and non-tooling. The finest tooling leather is known as calfskin. It is of medium thickness, comes in all colors, and is suitable for making billfolds, purses, and accessories. Several cheaper grades of leather come in the same thickness, two of which are kip and sheepskin. Cowhide is a thick tooling leather used for such objects as belts, knife sheaths, and briefcases. Because of its thickness, designs are usually carved on the surface. Non-tooling leathers, such as ostrich, pigskin, lizard, alligator, are decorative in quality and require only creative design to make pleasing articles. We must mention another type of leather called skiver which is used by most leather craftsmen. It is a very thin hide that is used for linings. It comes in various colors and is inexpensive.

Minimum Tools for Leather Work

With the tool outfit pictured on the opposite page, all of which can be purchased at a minimum cost, you will be able to do almost any kind of leather work.

The modeler, consisting of spoon and tracer, will serve for tracing and tooling designs on your leather. The tracing end comes in handy for other things, too—drawing lines, etc. The snap button fastener is for setting snap fasteners and is indispensable. There is a 6" steel rule, as you see. It is for measuring and marking off the leather.

In addition to these things, you will have to have a working surface. A hardwood board in a size large enough for cutting out handbags, book covers, or portfolios makes a good portable worktable. Keep one side smooth for tooling, and on the other do your cutting and pounding. (If there is a glass slab around, you can use that for a tooling surface.)

Making a Key Case. We have chosen a key case because it involves almost all the operations used in leather work. After you have made one of these, you will be able to forge ahead into advanced work.

The first thing to do is to cut a paper pattern. The size is a matter of your own taste and convenience. There are two points especially to be noted. The marks on both sides of the key plate indicate that you must allow some material here for the fold-over—1/4" on each side. Also allow for the overlapping of the ends. Rounded corners and a scalloped edge for the overlap make a nice finish.

Lay your paper pattern on the leather. You can use a little rubber cement on the corners to hold it in place. Learn to be economical in laying on your pattern. Leather scraps can be utilized for buttons, book markers, and small purses, but don't cut into your material until you have figured how to get the most out of it.

Put your ruler on the edge of the pattern and draw an outline with a pencil or with your tracer. Cut it out with a knife or a pair of scissors. If you use a knife, hold the steel rule firmly at the outline while you cut; this will guide and steady your knife and give you a clean edge.

Next cut an extra piece of leather on which to mount your key-plate. (Key-plates, by the way, can be purchased at craft stores. They hold from three to six keys.) The leather mount should be about $3/4''$ wider and $1\frac{1}{2}''$ longer than the plate. If you like, you can make it long enough to be laced in at the bottom. This will make the case a little firmer.

Draw a design on paper and transfer it to the right side of the leather for tooling. If you haven't an idea at the moment, perhaps you can find a decoration that appeals to you somewhere else in this book. But don't make an exact copy of anything. You'll enjoy your work more if you put some imagination into it.

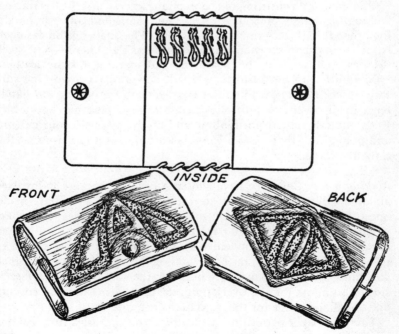

INSIDE

FRONT

BACK

Moisten the leather all over on both sides with a sponge but be careful not to soak it. The design draft will adhere to the damp hide while you are tracing it. Use the tracer end of the modeler, and impress the design firmly into the leather. (If it dries while you are working, moisten it again, and go all over it, front and back, each time.)

The first step in the actual tooling is to deepen your outlines with the tracer. Next, with the spoon held sidewise, follow the outline—the edge of the tool should rest in the dent. Press down and away from the outline toward the center of the background. Go around the whole outline this way, to throw the design into sharp relief, and then go over the background area with the spoon. When making your outline deeper with the tracer use a sort of push-and-pull stroke. This keeps it even and prevents it from looking gouged in places. If you are stippling part of the design, use the tracer end. For any place where the design is to be impressed deeply, and where there is a large area, use the spoon.

Before attaching the key-plate to the extra piece of leather, make holes along the top edge with the rotary punch (the small hole) where it will be laced into the case proper. Place the key-plate on the mount and make a pencil mark where the eyelets must go. Then punch the holes. Push the metal eyelets through from the plate to the back of the mount. Then turn it over, use your eyelet setter, and flatten it out by giving the end of the setter a blow with the mallet.

Mark the place where the snap fastener is to go, punch the holes, and put in the button part first. The fasteners come in four parts. The hollow metal piece which fits over the snapper is put over the larger end of the snap-setting device, after pushing it as far as it will go through the hole in the leather and into the button. Cover the button or the end of the mallet with a piece of leather or cloth to avoid scarring the button. Give one smart blow with the mallet to set the button. The button usually goes on the right-hand side of the case.

Fold over the lap and make sure that you have marked the right spot for the other part of the fastener. You will see how it has to go, and also that the smaller end of the setting device is made to accommodate this part of the fastener. Use the little steel gadget that comes with the ruler. Place it over the snap projection, and give a blow with the mallet. A second blow here is liable to flatten out the fastener, so try to gauge your stroke nicely.

Your key case is now all finished but the lacing.

Stitching or Lacing

You must first punch holes along the edges to be laced. If you are going to lace together two pieces of leather of equal thickness, you must "scive" them down enough towards the edge so that when glued together they will be no more than one thickness. You do this with your knife. Trim the edges if they need it. They must not be ragged.

Cement the leather mount to the outside of the key case before beginning to lace. To make sure that the holes will match, make a pencil mark for them, and work from that point in punching the rest of the holes.

Use your steel rule and a pencil or the tracer to draw a line for your holes. The depth of the lacing depends on the article—the size and the wear and tear it may have; ⅛" or ³⁄₁₆" from the edge will be about right for fine work. The holes should be ⅛" apart.

A tool which is helpful here, but not absolutely necessary, is a three- or four-pronged marker or a tracing wheel. Either of these will make marks to guide the rotary punch so that your holes will be evenly spaced. (If you want to invest in an additional tool, there is a gauge punch which is very useful. It marks the place for the next hole, as it punches.)

The illustration on page 87 shows ten ways of lacing leather. There are still more lacing stitches, but these are the most important. The most commonly used are the Single-Strand Running Stitch, the One-Strand Spiral or Whip Stitch, the Loop Stitch, and the Saddle Stitch. If you do much leather work you will eventually need to know all ten.

The amount of lacing needed varies with the different stitchings, the depth of your border, and the thickness of the leather. For the Single-Strand Running Stitch allow about one and three-quarters times the border measurement; for Spirals, about two and a half times.

The Saddle Stitch takes two and a half times your measurement. You can use waxed linen thread for this type of stitching, and you will need two upholstery or leather-working needles.

For the other types of lacing you must allow five or six times the border length.

The Venetian Spiral or Whip calls for a soft, pliable lacing about ¾" wide. Lacings are usually calf or goatskin but there is plastic lacing which costs less.

In doing lacing, keep the inside of the work toward you and work from left to right. For a small article, have your lacing in one piece.

STITCHING OR LACING

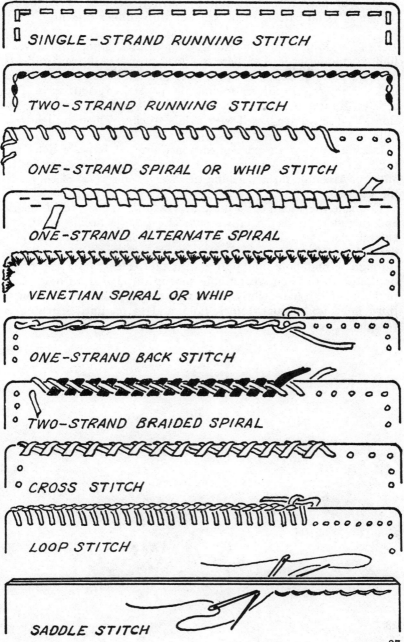

SINGLE-STRAND RUNNING STITCH

TWO-STRAND RUNNING STITCH

ONE-STRAND SPIRAL OR WHIP STITCH

ONE-STRAND ALTERNATE SPIRAL

VENETIAN SPIRAL OR WHIP

ONE-STRAND BACK STITCH

TWO-STRAND BRAIDED SPIRAL

CROSS STITCH

LOOP STITCH

SADDLE STITCH

87

If you make large things, however, you will have to divide your lacing and join it. You do this by sciving the ends to be joined (about ¾″) and pasting them together with rubber cement.

A Leather Project. If you are working with a group and have a limited amount of leather, here is a good project. Ask your students to cut a piece of paper 4″ by 12″ and plan an article they wish to make. They can do this by folding the paper in various ways. The articles illustrated on the opposite page will give you some suggestions. The seams are closed with saddle stitches, which are made as follows:

Draw a line ⅛″ in from outside margin and indicate holes for the stitches. This is best done with a spacing wheel, six notches to an inch. Assemble the article and tie together in several places ready for stitching.

To make the stitch, cut a piece of waxed thread a yard in length and thread a needle on either end. Use a large needle or awl to enlarge the holes. Push one needle down through first hole and draw thread through to halfway point. Now bring same needle up through second hole and pull thread taut. Next, push the other needle down through second hole and up through third hole, then pull thread through tightly. Push the other needle down through third hole, up through fourth hole, and so on until stitching is completed.

A LEATHER PROJECT

EACH ARTICLE CAN BE CUT FROM A 12"x 4" PIECE OF LEATHER

BILL FOLD WITH COIN PURSE

CIGARETTE CASE

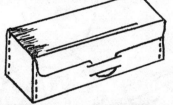

FIRST AID OR SEWING KIT

TWO-POCKET PURSE

ADDRESS BOOK

NAMES

MONEY PURSE FOR BELT

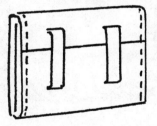

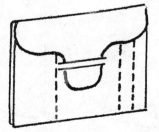

COMB AND FILE CASE

SADDLE STITCH

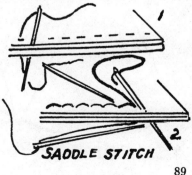

PROJECTS FROM SCRAP LEATHER

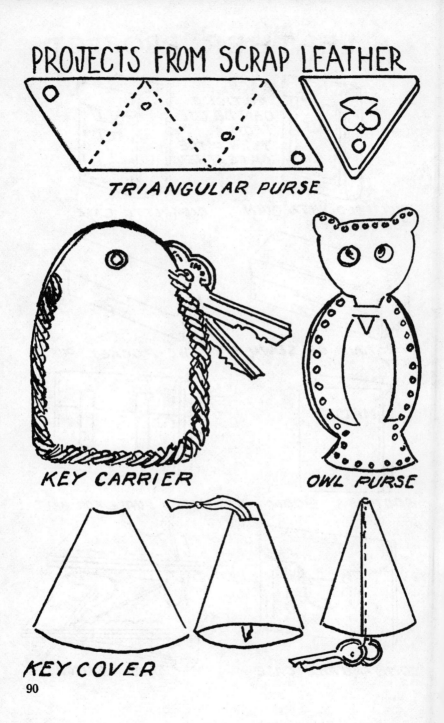

TRIANGULAR PURSE

KEY CARRIER

OWL PURSE

KEY COVER

CARVING LEATHER

Leather carving differs from other methods of tooling leather because all of the outlines of the pattern are cut vertically through one-half the thickness of the leather. The backgrounds are heavily stamped. Elaborate and conventional flower designs are traditional patterns. Saddles, bridles, belts, and holsters of the Southwest are examples of carving, but craftsmen have been adapting the designs and method to handbags, belts, book covers, and sandal straps. Cowhide is used.

Figure 1 shows a swivel knife, with which the vertical cuts are made. Other tools are a spoon modeler and background stamps. Dampen the leather and transfer your design to it. Cut around the major parts of the pattern with the swivel knife, and further open these cuts with the modeling tool. Use the background stamp to lower all of the background (Fig. 2). A wooden mallet is used to strike the stamps with fairly sharp blows. Finally, use the modeling tool to sculpture or round out the raised parts of your design (Fig. 3). Veins in leaves are made with the narrow end of the modeler (Fig. 4).

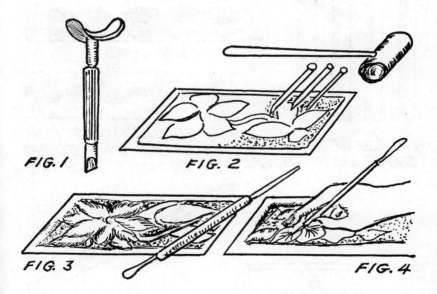

FIG. 1   FIG. 2

FIG. 3   FIG. 4

COW HIDE BELT

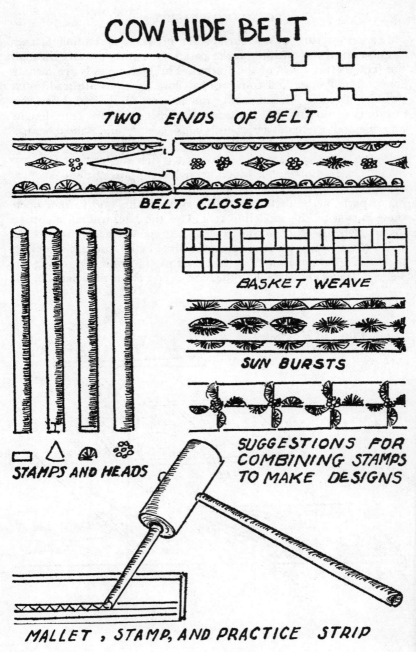

TWO ENDS OF BELT

BELT CLOSED

STAMPS AND HEADS

BASKET WEAVE

SUN BURSTS

SUGGESTIONS FOR COMBINING STAMPS TO MAKE DESIGNS

MALLET, STAMP, AND PRACTICE STRIP

COWHIDE BELT

Cut a strip of cowhide 2½" longer than waist measurement and the width of desired belt. Cut a pointed end on right-hand end, and four ¼" squares on other end as indicated in the drawing. Now cut out a triangle about 1½" from the point. The distance from base to apex of the triangle should be a shade longer than width of belt. By drawing the opposite end of the belt down through the triangle sideways and then turning it straight, the belt will be held in place without a buckle.

Wooden Background Stamps

Select ½" dowel stick and cut into 6" lengths. Trace on one end the design you wish to make—rectangle, square, half circle, or parallel lines. Cut away the background with a sharp knife, and smooth on a sanding machine. Be sure the design is outlined with a clear, sharp edge. By using a larger dowel stick, a more elaborate design may be cut for use in decorating the center of the belt.

How to Apply Stamps

Moisten the belt until it is thoroughly damp. Smooth the outer edges with a modeler or edge creaser. Next, decide on a border. It may be a parallel line within ¼" from the edge, or you may make a repeated design with one of the background stamps. To make a print with a stamp set in it, place on the damp belt and strike it a heavy blow with a wooden mallet or hammer. In order to set the stamp exactly, make an exact drawing of outline of design on top of dowel for a guide. This will enable you to set the stamp to carry out a design.

Another use that can be made of the wooden background stamps is to stamp down a background around a carved leather design. This process is described under "Carving Leather."

After the decoration is completed, allow the belt to dry thoroughly, give it a coat of paste wax, and when dry, polish it with a wool cloth. Add another coat, and repeat rubbing. The palm of the hand makes an excellent polishing tool.

Background stamps as a leather decoration are excellent for use with young children. Young fingers haven't the strength to push down leather with a modeling tool, but they can hit a dowel stick with a hammer.

SANDALS

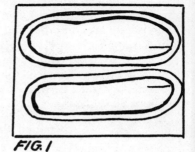

FIG. 1

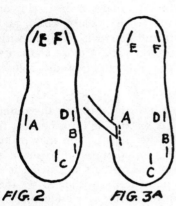

FIG. 2   FIG. 3A   FIG. 3B   FIG. 4A   FIG. 4B

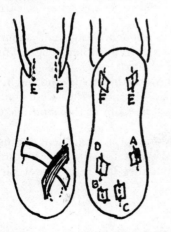

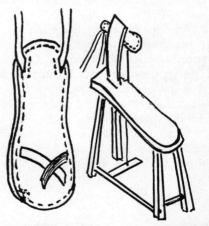

FIG. 5   UNDER SIDE   UPPER SIDE   HORSE

94

SANDALS

Draw an outline of each foot on a heavy piece of paper for a pattern. Be sure to draw a line between the great toe and the one next to it (Fig. 1). Cut out the patterns and lay them on a piece of fairly heavy leather. Draw a line around these ⅛" outside the pattern. Draw the line between the toes. Cut around the outline with a sharp leather knife. Do not cut between the toes. Remove the pattern and mark the points A, B, C, D, E, and F, making 1⅛" lines. Cut these slits with a sharp knife. These are for the straps that hold the sandals on the foot (Fig. 2).

Make the toe straps from calfskin. Cut the one marked AB ¾" wide, and long enough to cross the foot with 2" additional for sewing. Fit the strap across the foot and put 1" of the strap through slit A, with the end toward the middle of the sole. Sew it as shown in Figure 3A, using a saddle stitch (see page 88). Use an awl to punch the holes for sewing. Next draw the strap across the foot to slit B and put end B in the slit. Sew it in place with the end toward the middle of the sole (Fig. 3B). Cut the other toe strap CD long enough to reach across the great toe. Allow 2" extra for sewing. Fit the ends in the slits as indicated and sew in place. Cut two ankle straps, each 24" long and 1" wide. Fit them in slits E and F, slanting them toward the back (Fig. 5). Sew them in place. For the stitching, use shoemaker's linen twine and blunt shoemaker's needles.

For the soles, cut two pieces of sole leather to fit the sandals. Cement the outer soles to the sandals with rubber cement to keep them in place during the sewing. Use an awl to make holes ⅛" apart, and sew with a saddle stitch. Keep the sewing ⅛" from the edge.

An old-fashioned harness sewing horse is best for holding the sandals while sewing, but they may be clamped in a vise. To make the sandals fit well, dip them in water, put them on your feet and wear them for a couple of hours. You will really have your footprints in leather.

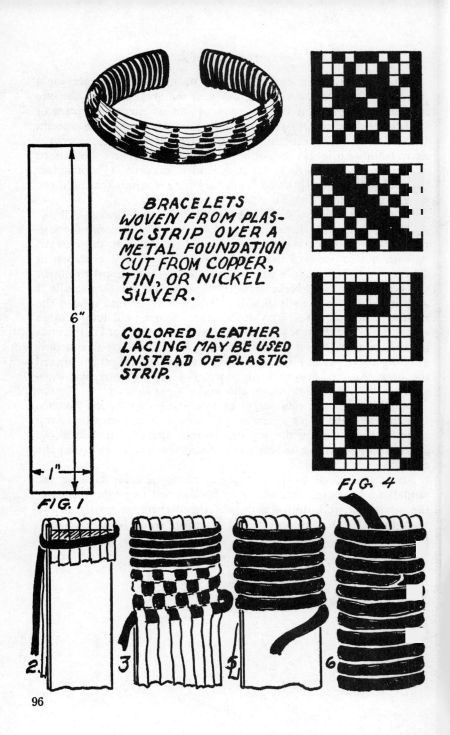

BRACELETS WOVEN FROM PLASTIC STRIP OVER A METAL FOUNDATION CUT FROM COPPER, TIN, OR NICKEL SILVER.

COLORED LEATHER LACING MAY BE USED INSTEAD OF PLASTIC STRIP.

6"

1"

FIG. 1

FIG. 4

2. 3 5 6

96

WOVEN BRACELETS

A woven bracelet is inexpensive, easy to make, and produces pleasing results due to a choice of many colors. It is made by weaving a surface with ⅛" plastic lacing over a metal foundation.

First, cut a metal blank 6" long and ¾" or 1" wide. Tin, copper, or nickel silver can be used for this purpose. For best results, use two colors of plastic lace, a light and dark shade. Use the light color for the warp, or lengthwise strands, and the dark for weaving in the pattern. Cut seven light strips for a ¾" width, or nine for a 1" bracelet. Each strand is 8" long. The surface must be covered with an uneven number of warp strips regardless of the width, in order to weave around and around continuously with the long weaver. Now, cut a piece of plastic lace in a dark color, three yards in length, to be used for weaving in a pattern.

Arrange the light plastic strips over the front of the bracelet foundation so that 1" extends beyond each end. Bend the strands back over one end and hold in place with a band of scotch tape (Fig. 2).

Next, take the long dark strand cut for the weaver and let 1" extend down from top over short strands. Hold it firmly in place with forefinger and thumb of left hand, and begin wrapping from top down around and around six or eight times (Figs. 2 and 3). You are now ready to weave a pattern. Figure 3 shows small squares—an easy pattern for beginners. This is accomplished by going under and over every other strand, weaving from right to left. Pull the weaver taut, then carry it back under back of bracelet to right side again. This time weave under and over opposite strands. Continue in this manner until within 1" of bottom of bracelet.

To complete the bracelet, fold the ends of the light strips back over bottom end and hold in place with another piece of scotch tape. Now carry the dark strand to the end of bracelet and wrap it around and around the same number of rows as at the beginning. Force the end up under the wrapping with a sharp instrument and pull it tight (Figs. 5 and 6). Cut away the end and shape the bracelet to fit the wrist.

To make other patterns, work out a design on graph paper, including as many squares as the number of warp strands. The dark squares indicate the strands covered by the weaver. Otherwise, it is carried underneath the warp strands.

Twisted Pattern

These Indian-like designs are obtained by twisting two plastic strips in contrasting colors across the top of the bracelet. Cut a metal foundation and cover the top with strips of light plastic lacing as described in directions for woven bracelets. Fold strands back over both ends of bracelet and fasten in place with scotch tape.

Now measure $3\frac{1}{2}$ yards each of a light and dark shade of plastic strip. Arrange the strips so the light is directly underneath the darker one. Wrap them around and around the top end of the bracelet six or eight times, with the light strip underneath. Hold firmly in place at point of wrapping with left hand and twist the strands that are still arranged one on top of the other. Bring the twist down on front of bracelet, up across the back. Make a second twist and lay close to first twist. The number and direction of the twists determine the pattern. End the bracelet by wrapping the end to match the beginning.

Before beginning the bracelet, we suggest that you practice several numbers of twists before deciding on a design.

BRACELETS

Twist. To wrap, place dark strand on light strand and hold firmly together. Make two twists to right each time the strands are brought around to face the bracelet.

Parallel Design. Cover face of bracelet with parallel strands, alternating the colors. Make wrappings at ends and intervals as shown in the illustration.

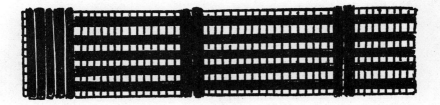

Braided. Cover bracelet blank with an even number of strands. Bind in place. Weave as indicated, leaving the center six strands free. Take center six strands in pairs of two, braid, and secure end of braid with other strands. Wrap end.

A BRAIDED LANYARD

Measure off as much cord as the finished length of your lanyard. Suppose it to be 16". You will need, then, for your work, two cords two and one-half times that length, or two pieces of cord or twine 40" long. Double your two strands and tie the loop ends with a piece of string, so that they can be hooked over a nail or a peg while you are braiding.

Spread out the four strands and cross 3 over 2 (Fig. 1). Next bring 4 *under* 2 and 3 and back *over* 3 (Fig. 2). Hold in place with left thumb and forefinger. Then bring 1 *under* 3 and 4 and back *over* 4 (Fig. 3). Again hold it in place with thumb and forefinger and continue braiding by bringing 2 *under* 4 and 1 and back *over* 1 (Fig. 4). Next take the outside cord on the left, which is 3, and bring it *under* 1 and 2 and back *over* 2. The braiding is continued by taking the highest outside strand, bringing it under the two nearest ones and back over the second one. In other words, the sequence is always under two strands and back over one.

When the braiding is completed, bring ends and loops together. Remove the small string around the loops and ravel out one small strand; wind this strand around the lanyard above the loops as in the first step shown.

Next cut a piece of braiding cord about 14" long. Make a 3" loop at one end of it. Hold the lanyard in the left hand and lay the cord with the loop to the left over the binding strand. The other end has a short cord and a long one. Begin winding the long cord over and over from right to left as tightly as possible. When you have wound about 1" pull the strand through the loop. Hold it with the fingers of the left hand. Grasp the short end of the cord and pull hard. The loop will disappear into the wound cord. Cut what's left of the cord and cement the ends.

Square braiding (Fig. 5) can be used as a slip knot on a lanyard. The braid is formed loosely around the shank of the lanyard so that it will slide easily on a round braid. This can be braided to the length desired.

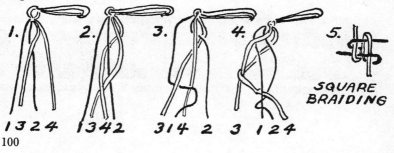

1.   *2.*   *3.*   *4.*   *5.*

SQUARE BRAIDING

1 3 2 4   1 3 4 2   3 1 4 2   3 1 2 4

BUTTONS AND BUCKLES

Buttons and buckles can be made from small pieces of wood. If you want to be creative, let the original shape of the piece of wood determine the design of the project. If you have no drill to bore holes in the buttons or beads, burn a hole with a hot needle.

Finishing the Wood

If you want a natural finish on the wood, sandpaper the surface until perfectly smooth, and wax it. However, you can improve this finish by adding a coat or two of shellac before the wax is added. The shellac acts as a filler for the wood. After the shellac is dry, rub the wood with fine steel wool or sandpaper. A coat of linseed oil will give the wood a mellow effect.

Color can be added in a number of ways. Delicate shades can be obtained with water colors. Oil paints are used when stronger colors are desired. Colored wax crayons may also be used. Color the object with the crayons, then rub gently with a rag on which a little machine oil has been poured. This will dissolve the crayons somewhat. If you rub it with a clean rag it will take on a sheen, due to the wax in the crayon.

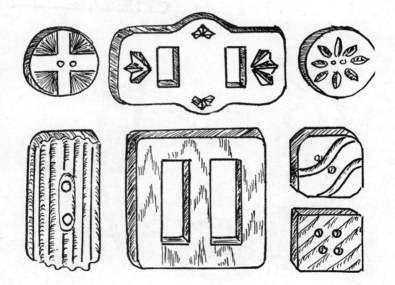

ONE-FRAME LOOM

FIG. 1

FIG. 2.

ONE-FRAME LOOM

This simple loom is excellent for teaching the beginning steps in weaving. The equipment includes a single frame, shuttle, beater, and a stick at one end for attaching to the waist.

How to Construct Frame

The frame can be made in any width, depending on the articles you wish to weave. Select two long pieces of wood 1" wide, and cut a groove ½" deep on one side. The reeds are made of splints and tongue depressors. Drill a hole in the center of each splint and three holes in each tongue depressor. Now fit the reeds in the grooves of the two long pieces of wood and glue them in place. Alternate one tongue depressor with every two or three splints.

How to String Loom

A wool yarn such as hand-knitting worsted is most satisfactory for weaving on this loom. Cut each strand about twice the length of article you wish to make, to allow for extra thread needed at the end. Thread a strand through each hole in the frame and also one between the splints and tongue depressors. Now tie the strands at one end to a stick 8" to 10" long, to be attached to the waist.

How to Weave

Make a shuttle, and wind on yarn for your weft thread. Attach the warp strands on one long stick to your waist, and tie those on the other side of the frame to back of chair (Fig. 2). Now push the frame of loom down. This will force the strands in the holes down and those between the reeds up, thus forming a shed or open space for the shuttle. Carry the shuttle through the shed from right to left, and leave a weft thread lying diagonally across the warp threads on the bottom. Push this thread back along the stick at the waist with a thin stick the width of the weaving, known as the beater. Now pull the weaving frame up. This will bring the threads in the reeds above those in between the reeds and form another shed. Pass the shuttle back across, this time going from left to right. Push the thread back against the first weft thread with the beater. Continue passing the weft thread back and forth until article is completed.

The three holes in the tongue depressors bring three strands through the weaving, which give the appearance of a heavy cord. If you prefer a plain weave, simply bring thread through one hole and ignore the other two.

WOVEN ARTICLES

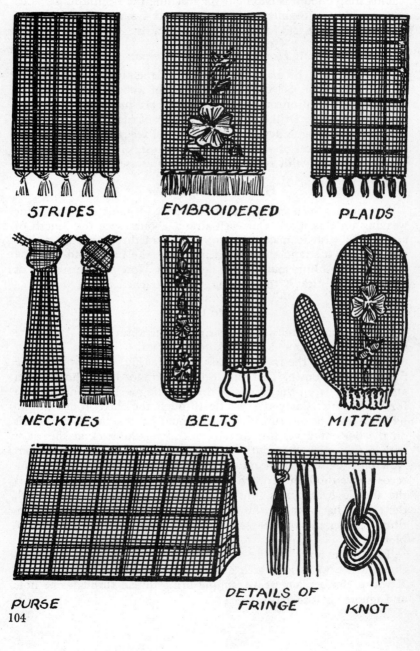

STRIPES

EMBROIDERED

PLAIDS

NECKTIES

BELTS

MITTEN

PURSE

DETAILS OF
FRINGE

KNOT

104

TWO NOVEL BELTS

Crocheted Ring Belt. Small brass rings may be purchased at any ten-cent store. Cover them by crocheting yarn or silk cord around them with a single crochet stitch. It is also possible to add the covering by bringing the thread around the ring and up through loop at top without using a hook, as in a buttonhole stitch. Assemble the covered rings in rows and attach with a matching thread. The belt is most effective when several colors are used.

STITCH

BELT, FIG.1

Clothesline Belt. Cut a piece of clothesline twice length of belt—plus 4″ for making a loop at each end. Cover the rope by winding yarn or silk cord around and around it, as shown in the illustration. Now fold it in half and fasten the two strands together with strips of leather or felt placed at intervals of several inches (Fig. 2). To finish the belt, bring one strand of the other end around to form a loop and fasten the end under the connecting piece of leather or felt. Add a cord to each end for tying to the waist.

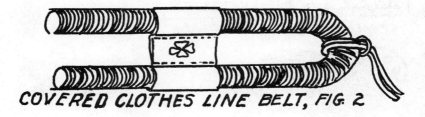

COVERED CLOTHES LINE BELT, FIG. 2

SEQUIN JEWELRY

The materials needed for this craft include small pieces of felt, sequins, celluloid, seed beads, thread, and a thin needle.

Cut a piece of celluloid in shape of article you wish to make. Make a pattern about 1/4" larger all around, and cut a piece of felt this size. Now arrange the sequins over the top in a pleasing design. Sew them to the felt by bringing the needle up through the hole, string on a small glass bead, and push the needle down through the same hole. Continue this operation until all sequins are attached. If you are covering a large surface, make the center design first, then add the sequins around the outer edge. Fill in the center last.

Lay the felt over the celluloid foundation and turn in the edges. Sew in place by bringing the needle back and forth across the back. Now cement a pin or ear clip to the back with Duco cement.

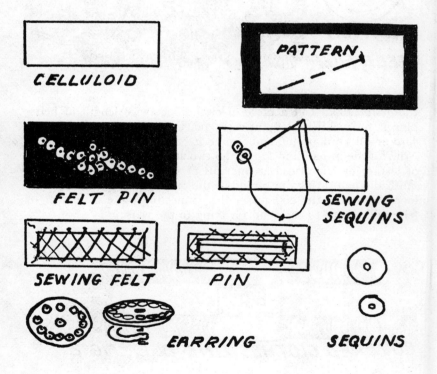

CHUNKY JEWELRY

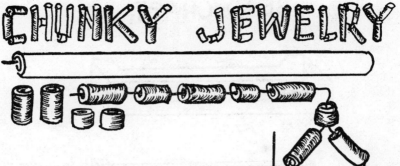

This iridescent jewelry is fun to make and can be worn with summer dresses. It is most useful when used with costumes in a stage production. If used for this purpose, the size should be exaggerated.

The jewelry is made by rolling cellophane into a long tube. Then cut into units as shown in the illustration. It should be rolled over a thin rod or dowel to form a hole in the center. Cut the cellophane sheets in two or three parts before rolling; it is difficult to roll it tightly if the tube is too long. When the roll is completed, secure the edges with Duco cement. The illustrations suggest ways of stringing the tubes.

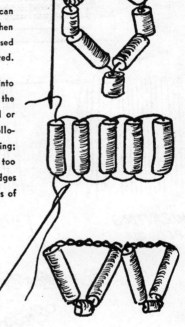

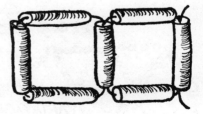

BEAD CRAFT

FIG. 1

BEAD LOOM

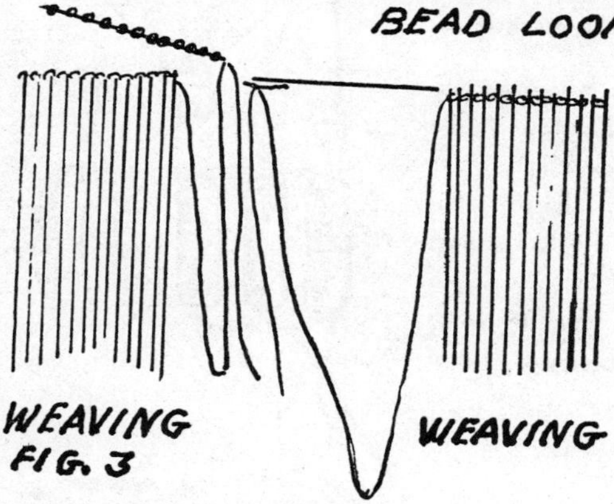

WEAVING
FIG. 3

WEAVING

FIG. 2 DESIGN

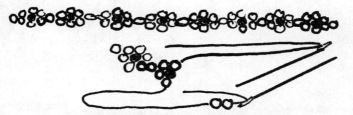

FIG. 4   FORGET-ME-NOT

FIG. 5   VARIATIONS FOR BEADS

BEAD CRAFT

Beads are most commonly woven into strips on a small loom. Several types of looms are sold commercially, but you can make your own. Make a wooden frame 6" by 12", and 3" deep. Cut away the sides as shown in Figure 1. Cut the notches on one end at the top for attaching warp threads. Begin at the right-hand notch, having a knot in the end of the thread. Wind the thread by passing it lengthwise over the opposite end down and under the frame and up and over the notched end. Continue wrapping in this way until the desired number of threads are strung lengthwise on the loom. Be sure that there is one more thread than the number of beads to be used in the width of the pattern. On the last string, tie a knot on the end to slip in the left-hand notch. This holds the warp secure.

To design a pattern, use graph paper with 1/8" blocks. Count one square for each bead. By using colored pencils to indicate the colors of the pattern, the design is easily followed. Figure 2 shows design for a repeated motif. Letters, flowers, leaves, and geometric arrangements lend themselves to bead weaving.

Figure 3 shows how to begin the weaving. Use a thin bead needle with fine strong thread. Tie the thread, as indicated, to first warp thread on the right. String the number of beads needed for the first row, carry the beads and thread under the warp toward the left. Set each bead between a warp thread, pull the bead string fairly tight, bring the bead thread up and over the left warp string, and run the needle through each bead toward the right. Repeat, picking up the beads needed for each row.

Forget-me-not Chain (Fig. 4) uses two needles and no loom. Cut a thread about a yard long. Thread a bead needle on each end. To begin, thread one bead and place it at the middle of the long thread. Next, thread two beads on the right-hand thread and run the left-hand thread through them. Pull both threads tight. The third step is to thread three beads on the left-hand thread and run the right-hand thread through them toward the left. The middle bead is usually yellow, to form a center for the flower. Pull these threads tight. Put two beads on the left-hand thread, pass the right-hand thread through them, and pull the threads tight. Last, put one bead on the left-hand thread, run the right-hand thread through it, and one flower is complete. Repeat until the desired length is made. Figure 5 shows other variations of stringing beads.

FEATHER JEWELRY

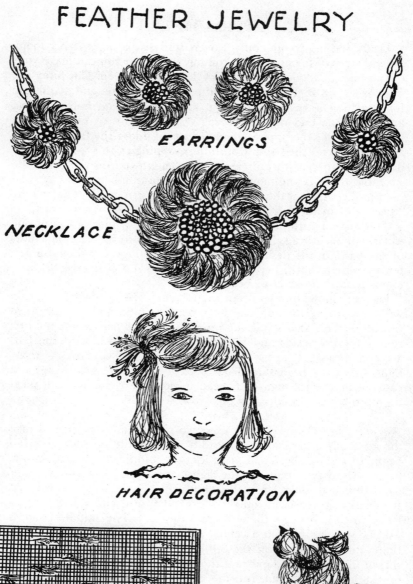

EARRINGS

NECKLACE

HAIR DECORATION

WEAVING

CHICK

FEATHER JEWELRY

If care is taken in selecting feathers and assembling them correctly, attractive costume jewelry can be made.

Use fine, soft feathers, such as down, and try to match them as to size. You probably will want to dye them a special color, which must be done before making the jewelry. Feathers are usually covered with a protective oil which resists water and must be removed before placing them in the dye bath. If the feathers resist the colors, proceed as follows:

How to Dye Feathers

Make a solution of one pound of lime to one gallon of water. Stir thoroughly and allow to stand several hours. If some of the lime has settled on the bottom, pour off the clear liquid into another container, and immerse the feathers. Allow them to remain in the bath three days, then rinse thoroughly in warm water. Place them in the dye, rinse them, put in a cheesecloth bag to dry. Hang the bag on a line and beat feathers with a stick occasionally so they will be fluffy when dry.

How to Make Jewelry

Two round plastic discs are used for the center. Cover the face of one with Duco cement and arrange the feathers in place around the edge. Note that they overlap somewhat in the illustration. Now add some more Duco cement and place the second disc on top. Cement small yellow beads over the top, to resemble the center of a flower. Add metal findings, such as clips or pin backs, by cementing them to disc at back. Pierce both discs on either side for attaching necklace chain.

Boutonnieres or hair decorations may be made by tying a group of feathers into a center with fine wire. Small glass beads are strung on wire and added for centers.

The down, when colored, may be woven into fabrics on a loom. Be sure that the quill is imbedded in the weft.

Tiny chickens for Easter are made by gluing the feathers to a small cork. Wire legs are attached, and little pieces of felt make a beak and eyes.

PLASTIC JEWELRY

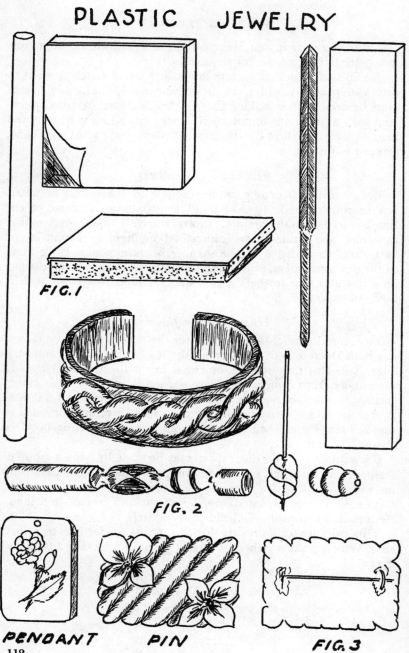

FIG. 1

FIG. 2

PENDANT   PIN   FIG. 3

PLASTIC JEWELRY

Plastic jewelry is simple to make and even small children can make their own pins and bracelets. Since many of the pieces require very little plastic, they can be made from scrap found around the craft shops. Three forms of plastics are usually used for making jewelry: flat pieces $\frac{1}{4}''$ in thickness, small rods, and hollow tubes.

Jewelry from Flat Pieces. Plastics usually come with paper on both sides to keep the surface from being scratched. On this paper, draw an outline of the article you wish to make. Now refer to pages 36–37 which give detailed instructions for handling plastic. After you have completed your first steps in making pins, earrings, pendants, or bracelets, remove the paper and add a decoration.

Decoration. Etching on a design is a popular method used to decorate plastic. Plastic becomes white when scratched or scraped with a sharp instrument and has the appearance of frosted glass. Scratch around the outline of your design with a sharp needle, then scrape the inside with a razor blade or small knife. The design may appear in a white silhouette form; or you may etch the background and leave a clear design. Special plastic paints may be purchased, for adding color.

Shaping Bracelet. After the edges are smooth, place the bracelet blank in a pan of boiling water. Allow it to boil four or five minutes, then remove it and quickly bend it around a bottle or round mold. If you are not successful at first, re-heat and try again. Do the etching first if bracelet is to be decorated.

Design in Relief. Beautiful designs can be made by filing away the surface, so the design stands up in relief. This is done with a three-cornered file, using folded sandpaper or emery paper to remove file marks. The illustration shows the possibilities in these designs. Note that beads are made by filing before the individual beads are cut from the rod. Holes are made by forcing a hot needle through the center (Fig. 2).

Pin backs and clips are held in place by a plastic cement (Fig. 3). This may be Duco or acetate, according to the kind of plastic used for the article. You may cut away the strip that holds the hinge and fastener in place if it interferes with the design. Cement on the hinge and fastener separately.

SHELL JEWELRY

PREPARATION OF SHELLS
COATING WITH LACQUER

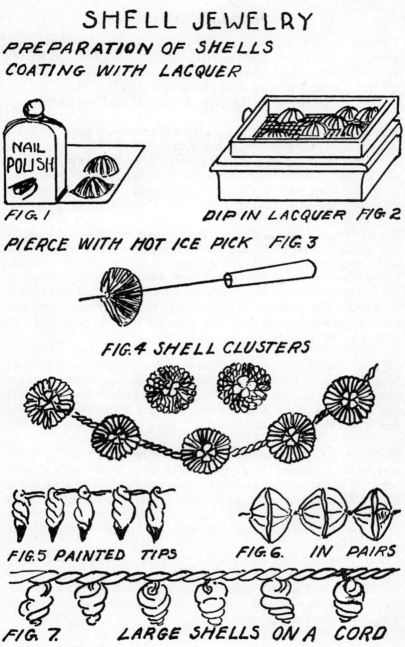

FIG. I

DIP IN LACQUER FIG. 2

PIERCE WITH HOT ICE PICK FIG. 3

FIG. 4 SHELL CLUSTERS

FIG. 5 PAINTED TIPS

FIG. 6. IN PAIRS

FIG. 7. LARGE SHELLS ON A CORD

SHELL JEWELRY

Shell craft has gained in popularity during recent years principally due to the fact that shells are now a commercial item. Packages of tiny shells in a great variety of soft colors can be purchased in any handcraft supply store. However, it is fun to find your own shells, dye them, and then design your own jewelry.

Ordinary dye will not penetrate the surface of the shells. It is necessary, therefore, to coat them with a thin coat of lacquer, allow it to dry, and then dip them into the dye. If you are planning to dye a few shells at a time, add a little thinner to clear nail polish and use it to cover the surface. For quantity dyeing, find a flat container and fill it partly full of thin clear lacquer. Now make a wooden frame that will fit into the container; tack a piece of fine wire screen to the bottom as shown in Figure 2. Cover the top with shells, dip into the lacquer, and set aside to dry. You are now ready for the dye baths.

If shells are to be used for jewelry, it is necessary to drill a hole at one end for stringing. This is difficult because of the curves at the top and bottom. It is possible to burn a hole by heating a sharp instrument such as an ice pick or a large needle (Fig. 3).

Shell Clusters (Fig. 4). The necklace and earring set is made by arranging tiny shells on a celluloid disc. They are held in place with Duco cement. Join several clusters together with a charm for the necklace, and fasten a clip to the back of the earrings.

Painted Tips (Fig. 5). Elongated shells make attractive necklaces if strung as shown in the illustration. Paint them any color you wish and add a darker tone at the top and bottom.

Shells in Pairs (Fig. 6). Shells strung in this manner make unusual bracelets and short necklaces. Paint the outside and give the inside a coat of darker color or a contrasting hue. Two colors or variations of the same color may be used on the outside. Make the outer edge one color and the center another.

Large Shells on a Cord (Fig. 7). Large shells are most effective if strung on a heavy cord an inch or more apart. They may be separated by knots. Add colo⁻ if you like.

SEED JEWELRY

HOW TO MAKE ROPE

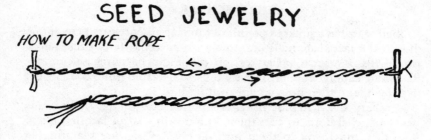

STRINGING SEEDS

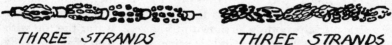

**THREE STRANDS
ONE BEAD BETWEEN**

**THREE STRANDS
TWISTED**

PEACH PITS

DATE PITS

PITS AND BEADS

SEEDS ON FORMS

SEEDS SEWED TO FELT

EARRING

PIN

SEED JEWELRY

Seeds grow in fascinating shapes and colors—one has only to gather them to have materials for jewelry for every costume. The seeds must be dried, sorted as to shape and size, and kept stored in a dry place. If the outside coat is not smooth and shiny, a coat of clear lacquer may be added.

It is necessary to make a hole in the seed if it is to be strung on a thread. Since a seed is soft in the center, the problem is to pierce the outer shells. Holes are usually made in small seeds by using a hot needle or ice pick, to burn through the surface. Large seeds, such as those found in fruit, are more easily pierced with a small hand drill.

How to Make Rope

Since seeds are most appropriately worn with sweaters or sport clothes, a wool or silk cord makes a good chain for attaching large seeds. It is very easy to make your own if you know how to twist rope. Cut a piece of yarn or cord eight times the length of necklace. Fold it in half and insert a small stick or pencil in loop at one end; then tie ends of the two strands to another small stick. Now grasp stick at loop end in your hands and ask a person to take the other end and stand facing you. Each one begins twisting the cord in opposite directions until the strands are entirely twisted. At this point, grasp the twisted cord at the center and bring the ends back to the loop on the stick. As you loosen your grasp on the rope, the four strands will twist together. Pull on the rope during the twisting so the spirals will fall into place.

The illustrations on the opposite page need no explanation. Creative designs can be made by alternating sizes and colors, making bead combinations, and adding color. Certain decorative knots are often placed between the seeds.

Earrings and pins are made by cementing seeds to a celluloid form with Duco cement. Add findings to the back with the same cement.

FLOWERS CUT FROM BREAD

This boutonniere is made of flowers and leaves cut from white bread. Cut individual leaves and petals somewhat larger than the flower you have in mind. Insert a thin wire up through the center of each leaf and bend it into a natural shape (Fig. 1). Cut the flower petals, leaving them attached to a center; attach a yellow bead to one end of wire stem and draw down through center (Fig. 2). Set the leaves and flowers aside to dry. When they are dry, color them with water-color paint or dye. Wrap the stems with narrow strips of green crepe paper, as shown in Figure 3.

To make the flowers and leaves more permanent, cover them with a coat of clear nail polish. Arrange them into a small boutonniere (Fig. 4).

FIG. 1   FIG. 2

FIG. 3   FIG. 4

FISH SCALE FLOWERS

Dainty flowers or motifs for costume jewelry can be made from fish scales. Select the largest scales and wash them thoroughly in water. While they are still wet, place them in an aniline dye bath which requires no heat. Remove them when they are the desired color.

As the scales are drying, try to shape them with your hands—some flat, some cup shaped, some turned back at the top. You may want to dampen them again as you work, depending on what you want to make.

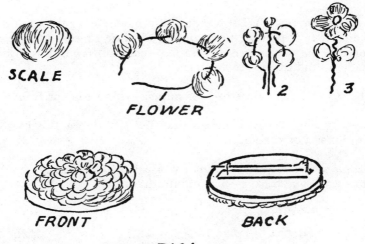

Small Flowers. If you are planning to make a bouquet of small flowers for an arrangement or boutonniere, use very fine wire for stringing the petals and for stems. Run the wire through the lower half of four or five scales for petals, and draw the wire tight to bring them into a circle. Fasten a yellow bead to end of another piece of wire, and draw down the middle to form center of flowers. Twist stems with green tissue paper. Add green scales for leaves.

Flowers can also be built up on a celluloid circle as a foundation. Glue the petals in place with Duco cement. The circle will provide a place to attach clips or pin backs.

119

ARTICLES FROM NECKTIES

Men's ties are made from beautiful materials such as brocades, satin, wool plaids, or cotton. Women have long used them for making silk quilts or afghans, but we think they can be put to other uses. Here are a few suggestions:

Ear Muffs (Fig. 1). Cut a foundation of buckram and line it with a soft warm material. Cover the top with bright woolen material cut from a tie.

Head Band (Fig. 2). Cut the foundation from buckram and cover with any fabric you wish to cut from a tie. Attach ribbon at each end for tying at back of head.

Glasses Case (Fig. 3). Use a beautiful brocade tie for the covering of the case. It is possible to restore an old case by cementing a new cover to the old surface. Use rubber cement if the case is made of leather. Bind edges with a silk tape.

Mittens (Fig. 4). Cover back of mittens with a top cut from a tie.

Evening Bag (Fig. 5). Select a beautiful silk tie for this bag; add sequins as a decoration.

Bedroom Sandal (Fig. 6). Purchase a pair of soles at a store. Make cross straps and back, as shown in illustration.

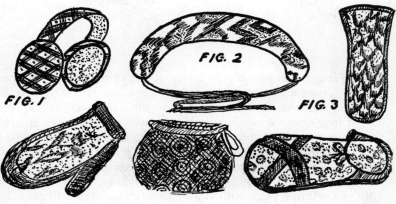

FIG. 1

FIG. 2

FIG. 3

FIG. 4

FIG. 5

FIG. 6

4

Crafts for Camps and Playgrounds

The crafts included in this chapter can be integrated into other recreational activities, such as dramatics, nature, music, or campfire entertainment. In the so-called recreational crafts anyone may participate, even though he has no interest in becoming a craftsman. He will be making something either for the fun of creating, or for special occasions.

The crafts we have selected as suitable for camps and playgrounds have another important characteristic—it is possible to complete them in a short period of time. This is important for playground, day camp, or an established camp that takes children for one or two weeks. The child will receive the greatest satisfaction because he can make something useful, integrate it with his special interest, and most important, complete the work.

An organized craft shop in a camp or playground is not only important for handling tools and materials but it can also be the focal point for all the craft activity. Projects can be handled both in the shop and elsewhere in the surrounding area. Those that require the use of water, more elaborate tools, mixing pots, etc., are best done where the equipment is handy. Other crafts that require few tools and use natural materials can be done outside the craft shop. With this type of planning, leaders can be trained to handle parts of this activity, and many children served. All tools handed out should be marked and a check system used for those who borrow them.

INDIAN CRAFTS

So many camps have Indian programs that we would like to make a plea for them to become a more serious educational experience in addition to being good entertainment. A child wraps himself in a blanket, wears a headband with a feather, gives a war whoop, and pretends he is an American Indian! Now we would like to ask how many tribes ever wore blankets to a council ring, what type of feather did an Indian wear and where was it placed, and how does a real war whoop sound?

The point we want to make is that any program which includes children should be authentic. Libraries have information about the different tribes—what they wore, type of headdress worn by the chief, dancers' music, types of campfires, and so on. The Department of the Interior in Washington, D.C., puts out numerous pamphlets covering all phases of the American Indians. Your own library may supply you with information about the tribe that lived in your own locality. Once you have collected the information, your program will be enriched with games, music, and crafts perhaps never before tried in a camp.

Indian designs are most interesting to use as decorations on many craft articles. Since most of them are symbolic, it would be interesting to learn their significance. Many designs are based on a circle, as the Indians worshiped the sun. The idea of the circle was carried out in many of their activities, in honor of the sun god. Just to mention a few—the council ring, round tepees, the drum or tom-tom, and the headband. Indian dances are usually danced in a circle, and their mode of warfare was to encircle the enemy.

Indian cooking is most appropriate for campers, as in earlier days everything was cooked over an open fire on hot rocks. Many of the recipes might not appeal to children but they would accept them occasionally just to learn what Indians used to eat. Since corn meal was one of the staple foods, children might grind their own meal between stones.

There is no limit to good material that can be incorporated into a camp program. The Indian lived out of doors and had the same activities as a camper. The question is—How did the tribes differ in customs, dress, etc.? This is what we hope you will want to discover.

INDIAN RATTLES

Rattles are used to produce rhythm effects in Indian dances. They are a round ball-like structure with a handle attached. They are held in the hand and shaken during the dance.

A Rawhide Rattle. Cut two circles of rawhide 5″ or 6″ in diameter. Soak them thoroughly in water to soften the material. While the circles are wet, sew the edges together with an overhand stitch, leaving openings at the top and bottom for a handle. Stuff the center as tightly as possible with grass, and allow to dry. Remove the stuffing, and put several small pebbles inside the rawhide "ball." Insert the stick for a handle as shown in the illustration. Decorate with Indian designs or symbols by using oil paints.

Gourd Rattle. Select gourds of the proper shape for rattles. Dry thoroughly and cut a small hole at the top. Insert small pebbles. Seal the hole with small strips of paper which have been dipped in paste, or use a small cork. To decorate the gourd, first wash it in alcohol, and then apply the designs with any kind of paint. If tempera is used, cover it with a coat of shellac. These rattles need not have a handle, as they are held in the hand and shaken.

INDIAN HEADDRESS

One of the most impressive events in a boys' camp is a campfire based on an Indian theme. Costuming is necessary for this, and most important is the headdress. Since each feather in it represents an honor won by the wearer, it should be worn by the chief of a camp tribe or any boy who has won many honors. The feathers can be prepared beforehand and presented as a ceremony at a previous assembly. Originally, most tribes used eagle feathers; later, white turkey feathers were substituted. By dyeing the tips of the white feathers brown or black, they closely resemble those of the eagle.

The crown of a felt hat or any boys' cap makes a satisfactory foundation to which the feathers are attached. Pairs of holes $\frac{1}{4}$" apart are punched all the way around the edge of the foundation. Keep the pairs about $\frac{3}{4}$" apart, 1" above edge in front and $\frac{1}{2}$" above in back (Fig. 1). Next, the feathers must be prepared. First, put a little glue on the lower part of the long feather shaft and arrange two or three fluffy feathers around it; tie in place with silk thread. Next, cut a piece of soft leather 3" long and $\frac{1}{4}$" wide, for a lacing loop. Fold and glue this to the shaft as shown in Figure 2. Leave a $\frac{1}{8}$" loop. Cut a narrow strip off red flannel and wrap around the ends of the leather and on up until the ends of the small fluffy feathers are covered. Use red silk thread to sew this in place (Fig. 3). The tip of the feather has a strand of horsehair attached to it with cement. Tie the strands together first with silk thread. A fluffy feather may be included in the strand for further decoration (Fig. 4). You will need about thirty feathers.

When the feathers are dry, they are ready to be attached to the foundation. Put the longest one in front and the shortest in back. Make each side even. Use a shoelace to hold them in place. Begin at the center front and put half of the lace through one of the holes in the center front, run it through the loop of the largest feather and back through the other hole in that pair. Draw it tight. Bring the lace out through the first hole in the next pair and through the loop on the next largest feather and back in the hole beside it. Take the other end of the lace and attach a matching feather on the other side of the center feather. Attach all of the feathers, matching each one on the left to one on the right. When you come to the center back with both laces, draw them tight and tie them. Another lacing 4" above this keeps the feathers upright. Make little holes in the shaft of the feathers; using linen thread and a needle, run the needle through the hole, around the back of the shaft, and into the same hole. Keep the feathers 1" apart. Attach lacing to the next feather,

124

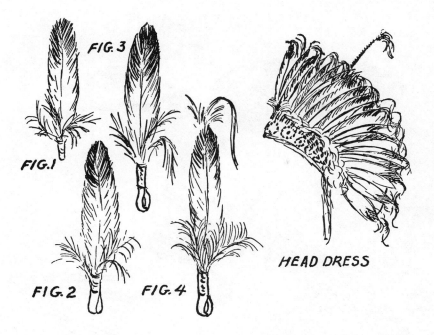

FIG. 3

FIG. 1

FIG. 2

FIG. 4

HEAD DRESS

and so on around the circle. Tie the thread to the feathers where you began. The plume or a feather for the center of the crown is made by using the shaft of a long feather which has been stripped. Bind a few fluffy feathers to its tip and put a loop at the lower end and sew it to the center of the crown.

A chin strap is made of two leather thongs attached at each side. Strips of rabbit fur are attached where the chin straps are fastened to the foundation. A strip of beadwork is sewn across the front.

INDIAN GAMES

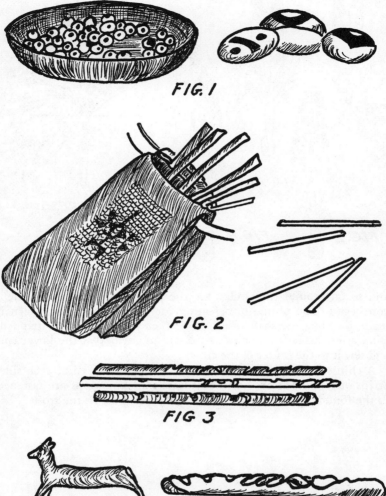

FIG. 1

FIG. 2

FIG 3

FIG. 4

FIG. 5

INDIAN GAMES

The American Indian is a great lover of games, particularly those having to do with sports and those based on the element of "chance." Since the Indians were great athletes, perhaps the favorite games included running, jumping, or shooting their bows and arrows. The rules for games of chance are not clearly described and were probably varied according to tribe or use.

The equipment used for games was fashioned out of natural materials such as sticks, seeds, bones, pebbles, or corn cobs. Color or small dots were added to identify pieces belonging to individual players. Small flat bowls or leather bags were used as containers. Many of the sticks were beautifully carved.

Since so many camps have Indian programs or campfires, we thought it worth-while to include the games illustrated.

Pebble Game (Fig. 1). This game of chance may be played by each player placing a certain number of small pebbles in a shallow bowl—each one's pebbles being marked differently with small dots or a color on one side. They are then poured out on the ground and the players count only the stones that land with decorated tops exposed. A similar game is played by using cherry pits.

Figure 2 shows a two-pouch bag made of doeskin held together with a strip of leather, and containing a number of small sticks. It was worn by hanging it over a belt at the waist. It was carried by a visiting warrior, who on arrival danced in the council ring. When he completed the dance, he scattered the sticks on the ground. The manner in which the sticks fell had certain significance, even to peace or war between the tribes.

A Bundle of Sticks (Fig. 3). Some tribes gave sticks as an invitation to ceremonies. The sticks were sometimes carved with symbols sacred to their tribe. This idea may be used in camps where each tribe designs its own invitation sticks.

Tokens (Fig. 4). Thin sticks of wood were often cut into shapes of animals or people; they were given away as tokens.

CORN COB DART

INDIAN GAMES

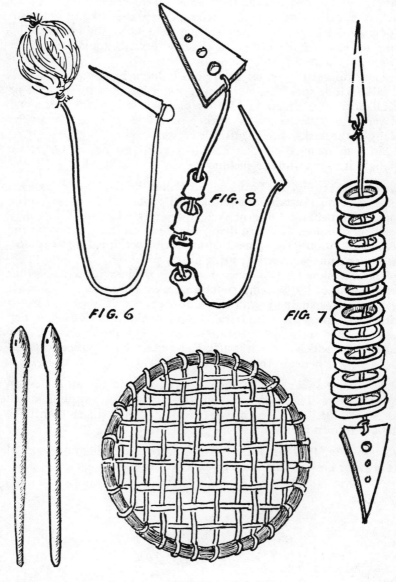

FIG. 8

FIG. 6

FIG. 7

FIG. 9

FIG. 10

Stick Game (Fig. 5). These sticks were carved on one side with designs that stood out in relief. They were held high above the head and dropped to the ground. The player whose stick landed right side up won.

Corn Cob Dart. Cut a piece 5″ or 6″ in length from the pointed end of a corn cob. Find three wing feathers, matching in size if possible. Place them equidistant at broad end of cob, setting them so they curve outward from the center. Use a large darning needle for the sharp end of the dart. Since the inside, or pith, of the cob is soft, remove some of it and replace it with plastic wood. Insert the head of the needle, and allow the plastic wood to dry before using the dart. See bottom of page 127 for illustration.

Zimba. There are many variations of the game, three of which are shown in Figures 6, 7, and 8. A sharp-pointed stick is attached to one end of a heavy cord or thong, and a triangular piece of leather or a bunch of grass is tied to the other end. The thong should be about 30″ long. If the leather triangle is used, two or three holes should be cut in it. The game is played by holding the stick in the right hand with the point extending beyond the thumb and forefinger. The leather triangle or bunch of grass on the opposite end of the cord is thrown forward from the body and then jerked back. As it comes back, the player attempts to pierce the grass with the point of the stick. If the leather is used, he tries to get the point of his stick in the holes in the triangle (Fig. 8).

Another version of the game uses ten rings of marrow bone cut very thin and strung as shown in Figure 7. The player gets one point for each ring that he caught on the stick, and ten points for each hole in the triangular piece of leather.

Snake Sticks (Fig. 9). Snake sticks were beautifully carved from lengths of wood into snake forms. They were several feet in length and 2″ in diameter. The game was played by hurling the stick along the top of the snow. The object of the game was to see who could send their snake stick the farthest. This game is adaptable to land or water activities.

Hoop Game. The players stand in two lines facing each other. A hoop is rolled down the middle of the space between them. Darts or sticks are hurled at the hoop, the object being to throw them through it as it passes. Sometimes the Indians wove a center in the hoop so the darts would pierce the threads and stay in place (Fig. 10).

129

INDIAN DRUMS

FIG. 1

FIG. 2

FIG. 3

FIG. 4

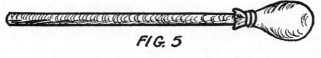

FIG. 5

FIG. 6

INDIAN DRUMS

The American Indians used drums to summon their tribesmen together in villages and ceremonials around a campfire. A smaller drum, known as a tom-tom, was used for beating rhythm for dances.

Regardless of the type or size, all drums were constructed with certain basic principles. The foundation must be hollow in order to produce a vibration to carry sound, so drums were usually made with a covering on either end. However, one head can be used if the center is removed and the bottom is hollowed in a concave shape. A circular piece of rawhide is used for the drumhead, and long rawhide thongs are used for the lacing.

How to Make a Drum

Select a round foundation the size drum you wish to make. You might use a small wooden keg, sides of a cheese box, or tin can, as suggested in the illustrations. Remove the top and bottom carefully so that all of the rims are even. Smooth with sandpaper or steel wool, then bind with a strip of 1" adhesive tape to protect the drumhead. You will need two circles of rawhide 4" wider than the diameter of the drum. These can be purchased at your local music stores. Now draw an inner circle on each drumhead 1" from the edge. Punch holes 2" apart on these lines for the lacing. Narrow strips of rawhide or leather thongs are used for the lacing.

Soak the drumheads in water overnight so that they are thoroughly wet. Lay one on a flat table top and set one end of drum in the center, leaving 2" of rawhide to extend beyond the edges. Lay the second head on top of the drum. Tie the heads together at four places equidistant, to avoid slipping. Use temporary strings for this. Begin lacing the heads on the sides by pulling the thong all the way through the first hole. Tie a knot to keep it from slipping through the hole. Make a diagonal lacing rather than bringing the thong straight up and down. When the rawhide is dry, designs may be added with oil paints.

Fig. 1—Cheese box used for a foundation with cross stitch lacing.
Fig. 2—Drum with one head over wooden chopping bowl. The bowl provides a concave base for vibration of sound.
Fig. 3—Drum made from tin can. The surface can be covered with bark to make it more realistic.
Fig. 4—Drum made from a small wooden keg.
Fig. 5—Drum Stick. Select a stick for a handle. Pad one end and cover with soft suede or deerskin.
Fig. 6—Large stationary drum made of hollow log or large tin oil drum.

SOUND INSTRUMENTS

In an Indian dance the clamor of old sleigh bells, attached to the ankles and at the waist, adds much to the enthusiasm. When worn on the legs, protectors of sheepskin should be placed under the straps, to prevent rubbing of the flesh. Figure 1 shows how to attach them to a strap.

You can make your own tin rattles and they too make considerable noise, which seems to be a part of the Indian dance. Cut a piece of tin (Fig. 2) and bend it into a horn shape. Thongs are knotted at one end and drawn up through the horn. Tie these in groups and fasten to a strap which is worn around the leg below the knees or at the waist (Fig. 3).

A water drum makes a pleasant sound which can be heard all over camp. To make one, use a small wooden keg; remove the top and replace it with a drumhead, which may come from an old drum or a musical supply store. Make it about 4″ bigger than the top of the keg. A hoop of wire slightly larger than the top of the keg is wrapped with soft leather until it fits closely enough to hold the head in place (Fig. 4). Fill the keg one-third full of water and it is ready for use. By varying the depth of the water, the tone can be changed.

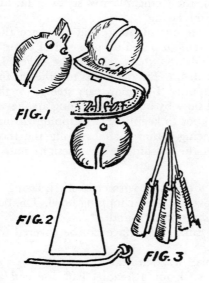

FIG. 1

FIG. 2

FIG. 3

FIG. 4

MUSICAL INSTRUMENTS

The Indians sang on many occasions. There were songs for court-
ing, which they played on a flute (Fig. 1) made from a piece of sumac
with the pith removed. Holes were bored at places on the sides.
There were dance songs which the Indians sang to the accompani-
ment of the whistle as they danced. A whistle can be made from a
chicken or turkey leg bone or a piece of bamboo. To make a bone
whistle, cut off the ends of a leg bone. Remove the soft center and
cut a triangular hole in the upper side with a small file. Make a stop
by forcing plastic wood through the opening. Shape the plastic wood
with the end of the file until the whistle makes the right sound (Fig.
2). Figure 3 shows completed whistle with decorations.

A willow whistle is made from a piece of willow about 1" in diameter and 4" long. Use green willow, preferably in the spring when
the sap is rising. Cut a triangular notch as shown in Figure 4. Next,
loosen the bark by tapping it with the knife handle, and the wood
can be slipped out. From the notched end of the wood, cut a plug
long enough to reach the edge of the hole in the back of the bark.
Cut a slice from the top of the plug (Fig. 5). Slip it back into the
notched end of the bark (Fig. 6). Slip the remaining piece into the
other end. By pulling this out at different lengths the tone can be
varied (Fig. 7).

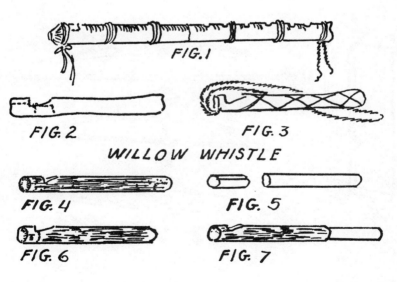

FIG. 1

FIG. 2   FIG. 3

WILLOW WHISTLE

FIG. 4   FIG. 5

FIG. 6   FIG. 7

FIRE BY FRICTION

A fire-by-friction set consists of four pieces: fire board, drill, bow, and drill socket. Red cedar is best for the board, which is ½″ thick, 3″ wide, and 12″ long. Cut notches and drill a small shallow hole at the point of each (Fig. 1). The drill is 12″ long and ¾″ square. Whittle the corners to make it octangular. Point each end as shown in Figure 2. The bow is made from a curved branch which is about 28″ long. A heavy thong is used for the bow string. Make it loose enough to go around the drill. Holes bored in each end of the bow make it easier to attach the string (Fig. 3). The drill socket, which is held on top of the drill to give pressure, is a piece of hard wood. Bore a 1″ hole half way through it. To make the drill run easily, fit a soda bottle cap into this hole (Fig. 4). In addition to this set you will need red cedar bark for tinder. Be sure that it is dry and shredded fine.

To make fire, lay the tinder on a chip of dry wood and set the fire board with a notch directly over it. Set up the drill, bow, and socket, as shown in Figure 5. Make long strokes with the bow and hold the drill socket on the top of the drill. Soon smoke appears and black powder drops into the notch. Slightly raise the board and blow the tinder to a glowing coal. By blowing gently, a flame will result. Move the flaming tinder and chip to your fire, which has been laid beforehand.

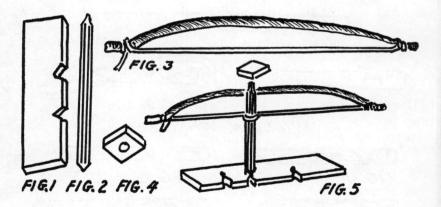

FIG. 3

FIG. 1 FIG. 2 FIG. 4 FIG. 5

THE CRAFT SHOP AND DRAMATICS

Dramatics are an important division of recreational activities, and in an integrated program the craft personnel will be able to make valuable contributions. To make the most of a dramatic production, the costumes and properties should be in keeping with the time in which the play is set. Since improvised equipment is likely to be used, the skill of the crafts person will complement the knowledge of the stage director. Properties are likely to be used only a few times; therefore, the least expensive materials may well be used. Tin, paper, cardboard, string, muslin, and old costumes yield satisfying results in the hands of a creative designer.

Marionettes and puppets have a great appeal for children. They not only involve fun and creativeness but are a means toward self-expression. Children forget themselves when they are manipulating these figures; therefore, how to handle them is a very important part of this craft.

The suggestions offered here are given with an idea of stimulating interest in the integration of dramatics and crafts. The possibilities are unlimited, and the projects given are intended as examples of what can be done in certain situations. Drama has many phases, such as charades, skits, plays, pageants, and festivals. Crafts play a part in all of them and can increase the value of such an activity.

Indian Program as a Group Project

An Indian program is suggested which utilizes both crafts and drama. The group may be divided into tribes, each tribe choosing and making shields to be carried in its grand council, which includes everyone. Each tribe may make authentic headdresses and plan a ceremonial featuring what each headdress symbolizes. The entire group may then prepare for the council which climaxes the work.

Following this may be a festival which uses the games and musical instruments prepared by the children. Having worked through from the original research to the actual presentation itself, the children will have a vivid and lasting memory of the Indians they represented. Besides which, they may have for their own some of the craft objects which they designed and made.

SOCK PUPPETS

These puppets were originated by Weaver Dallas for her Brer Rabbit shows. The entire puppet body is cut from a pair of men's socks. Besides the socks, you will need pieces of felt for features, shoe buttons for eyes, bits of fur and cotton to stuff the head.

The puppet body is cut from one sock, as shown in Figure 1. The toe is used for inner lining of head, where the three middle fingers are placed for manipulating purposes. Sew the two edges together, beginning at the top, and down to point where legs begin. See Figure 2B. Cut the arms, other half of legs and feet, ears, and outer head from other sock (Fig. 2A).

Sew the legs and feet to body cut from first sock; place a weight in the toe and stuff tight with cotton. Now sew arms together and attach to armholes. Do not stuff with cotton, as the thumb will fit into one and the little finger in the other, for arms. Next, sew the outer head together and stuff with cotton; shape it according to the animal you wish to make by sewing darts here and there. Add the ears, eyes, and other features. See Figure 2B.

The puppet is manipulated by thrusting the hand up through the body at the waist. Insert the middle three fingers into the head, and thumb and little finger into the two arms.

Select grey socks for a squirrel, brown for a bear, white for a pig, etc. Dress them in gay costumes, and add bits of fur for a tail.

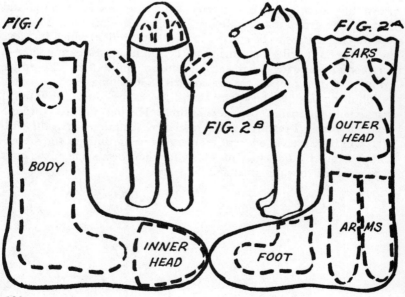

MR. SQUIRREL   MRS. PIG

PROPERTIES

137

BUFFOONS

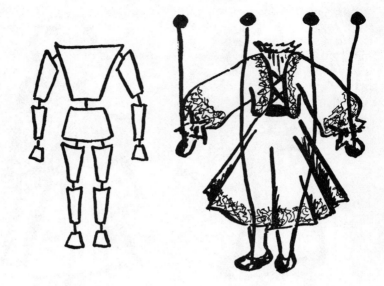

BUFFOONS AS A CRAFT

Buffoons are a simple way of presenting a show and need only a stage made by a standing frame covered with black cloth. Usually there are two persons who act the characters, so the frame should be big enough to cover the upper parts of their bodies. Their feet and legs are exposed below the frame. Holes are cut at the natural height for their heads and hands to protrude through the cloth. Small headless rag figures are attached below the holes cut for the heads. These bodies must be flexible at the joints, to permit manipulation by strings held in the hands of the performer. Attach a ring at the upper end of each string. His head forms the head of the figure, and he wears a hat or bonnet. The rag figure is dressed to suit the character represented. The lines of the play are written in dialogue form and spoken by the performers. To provide for different plays, a variety of costumes should be made for the figures.

A buffoon stage is an excellent property to keep in a recreation room for permanent equipment. It provides entertainment at parties when natural actors put on extemporaneous skits to amuse the guests. It is equally useful in a lounge or waiting room, where an occasional show will enliven conversation or relieve the monotony of waiting.

Carry the stage outdoors if a party is given on the lawn or playground. It will provide a corner where children can amuse themselves without a leader; it can become a photographer's studio—children love to have pictures of themselves as buffoons.

Buffoons are most spectacular when made to dance to musical rhythm. A special stage is constructed to set on the edge of a table so the buffoon dances on the table top. The legs must be well jointed and weights placed in the bottom of the feet. Strings must be attached to the knees, heels, and toes.

LIFE-SIZE PUPPET

This large puppet originated at a boys' camp. A puppet show had been suggested but there wasn't time, with all of the other activities, to make regular puppets. The large ones were made from paper cartons or orange crates. The sections were cut, and joined with heavy cord. Holes for the cord were punched in the cardboard with an ice pick. The puppets were dressed in the campers' clothes. The strings for manipulation were made of the heavy cord. A large needle was used to pass these strings through the clothes, to avoid holes which would damage the garments. Features were drawn on the faces. A tree limb was used for the support, as the illustration shows. Boys who manipulated the puppets were partly concealed by the box behind the puppets.

According to the story which the campers wrote about the events of the day, three boys worked each puppet and spoke the parts without memorizing the lines.

PANTOMIME PUPPETS

These puppets are flat figures cut from wood, tin, or cardboard. They are adapted from a type of puppet used by the Chinese, which was made of cardboard and the front dressed in elaborate costumes of fine silk. A little padding was added in the sleeves and headdress, to add to contour. If figures are to be cut from tin, decide whether they should be front or profile view. It is entirely optional with the group whether the figures are to be in silhouette form or dressed.

A small stage such as the one illustrated below is used for the production. At the bottom are two parallel tracks along which a 1" by 1" by 36" stick can be pulled—each going in opposite directions. Make ½" grooves in the top of each stick in which to insert the puppets. They are placed in the order in which they are to appear on the stage.

Since the puppets move in pantomime, the story is told by a member of the group. The characters move across the stage by pushing the sticks along the tracks. The scenery may be painted on a backdrop, or trees and houses may be placed in the stick and carried along with the puppets.

STAGE

STAGE PROPERTIES

TIN CHAIN

BELT FROM EGG BOX GILDED
WITH RADIATOR PAINT

TIN JEWELRY
COVERED WITH
CELLOPHANE

CROWN OF COPPER
SCREEN. JEWELS OF
GLASS BEADS. BIND
EDGES WITH GOLD TAPE.

CANDLE OF CARDBOARD
TUBE AND PAPIER -
MÂCHÉ

KNIGHT'S HELMET AND
GLOVE MADE OF TURKISH
TOWEL WITH RADIATOR
PAINT.

STAGE PROPERTIES

The making of stage properties and costumes is one of the most fascinating parts of dramatics. Since scrap materials are used to a great extent, the imagination is highly stimulated. A creative person thus may take part in producing a play, even though he has no desire to act.

In making stage properties, two things must be kept in mind: the size and the colors must be overemphasized. First, make a sketch of the set you wish to use and decide on color combinations. Next, make a list of properties that can be made in the craft shop, also jewelry or parts of costumes that can be created. Items such as candlesticks, trays, and sconces can be transformed into period pieces by covering them with papier-mâché and using suitable motifs and colors. After the play is over, the papier-mâché may be removed by soaking the articles several hours in water.

Here are a few ideas to get you started:

Tin Chain Links are cut from tin cans and shaped over a round form. It is not necessary to solder the links together, since there is no strain on them. Wrap the links with gold paper or cellophane if you want a gold chain.

Belt. This belt is made from strips of cardboard used for lining layers in an egg crate. Paint the surface with gold or silver radiator paint; add a buckle, also cut from cardboard.

Jewelry. Medallions or large jewelry pieces are most effective made from cellophane. For suggestions, turn to "Chunky Jewelry," page 107.

Crown. Crowns can be made from cardboard and gilded with gold paint. The illustration shows a dainty crown cut from copper screening. Bind the edges with gold passementerie tape, and add large beads or stones from costume jewelry, for jewels.

Knight's Costume. Helmets and gloves can be made from turkish towels covered with silver radiator paint, to imitate armor. The linings of egg crates may also be used for a helmet and belt.

Candle. A cardboard tube is fastened to a tin base. Cut an extra piece of tin for a handle. Cover the entire foundation with a layer of papier-mâché and paint it any color you desire.

PORTABLE SCREEN

A three-paneled screen is an excellent property for a camp dramatic group. Each panel is made of strips of soft pine easily inserted. Cover the surface with large sheets of plain paper, backed with cardboard if desired. Sketch on the scene you wish to make and paint in details with poster colors. It is a good idea to have children make their own scenery.

The screen can be spread out straight for a room interior, as shown in the above drawing. Figure 1, below, suggests a stone wall; a picket fence with flowers may also be used. Figure 2 shows a window opening in the center panel that can be used as a pay booth or puppet stage. A red and white striped awning can be arranged around the top to give the effect of a porch or patio (Fig. 3).

When not in use as a dramatic property, the screen makes a serviceable bulletin board for posting of notices or information. Also, the screen can be used as an oversized camp newspaper. Lettering is done in large letters so that it can be read by the entire group at one time.

LANTERN PARADE

Lanterns made from large cartons, illuminated with candles or a battery lantern, make an unusual show for an after-dark event. The sides are cut out in designs, and colored paper is pasted over the openings. Two people carry each lantern. One lantern may be used to advertise a coming event, in which case it can be set on a wall or any place where it is dark. Several lanterns used in a procession can be impressive. They are suitable for Halloween parades, or yard decorations for the same season. At Christmas they may have appropriate designs and be displayed in a yard or darkened window.

Use a large carton and draw a picture on each side (Fig. 1). Use a sharp knife to cut away the cardboard around the pattern. Save the piece which is cut out and on the other side of the lantern cut out a rectangle. Cover the opening with colored paper and paste the cutout figure on it for a silhouette. On the first side cover the opening with colored paper (Fig. 2). Set a candle in a small saucer or pan. Melt a little wax to hold the candle fast and also to hold pan in place. Set pan in bottom of carton. Cut a small opening in the top of the carton for a draft if candles are used for illumination. To carry the lantern, cut two holes in one end and two corresponding ones in the other end. Run long sticks through these for handles. (Fig. 3).

FIG. 1

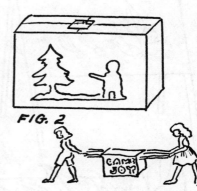

FIG. 2

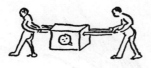

FIG. 3

FELTOGRAM FOR NATURE STUDY

CUT OUT PIECES OF FELT FOR BUILDING DESIGNS. SQUARES, CIRCLES, AND OTHER GEOMETRIC FIGURES ARE SUGGESTED.

ELM LEAVES AND SEED

ACORN AND WHITE OAK LEAF

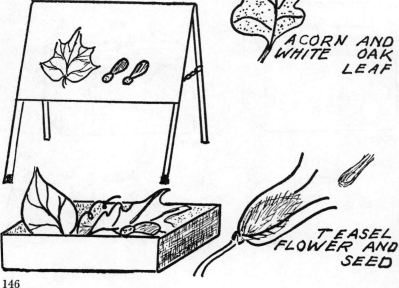

TEASEL FLOWER AND SEED

FELTOGRAMS

Feltograms are used primarily for storytelling or bulletin boards. They are made on the principle that felt adheres to felt when pressed together. A large frame is covered with felt as a background. Characters are cut from paper. A small piece of felt is glued on to the back. When they are pressed on the felt in the frame, they will stay in place.

EASEL   SCENES

For storytelling, we suggest you make the type of stage illustrated above. Cut two large pieces of cardboard, and hinge together by pasting a strip of muslin across the top. Cover the front and back with a piece of white felt. You may make a permanent stage setting by drawing a room scene on one side of the stage and a landscape on the reverse side. As a child tells the story, he places the character on the stage as it enters the scene.

Nature feltograms are educational and make good camp entertainment. Cut out pictures of flowers, leaves, birds, and related objects. Paste a small piece of felt on the back of each. As they are placed on the large felt background, ask the children to identify them. The children will enjoy originating their own games, such as matching a leaf with its fruit, or selecting flowers that grow near the water.

LITTLE RED RIDINGHOOD MEETS THE WOLF

INDIAN CHARM STRING

An Indian charm string can be the basis for a continuous craft program throughout the camping season. It is started by having each camper make an Indian charm for a friend. Later, these are presented at a "give-away" ceremony at campfire. This is most effective if all members of the camp form a large circle and dance to the rhythm of a tom-tom. First, each member, in turn, dances across the ring and presents his charm to a friend. This continues until everyone has received a charm. There is an old saying that the Indians gave the white men gifts but the white men gave them none in return, so the Indians took them back—thus the phrase "Indian giver." For this reason, every camper must reciprocate and return a charm for every one received. If this is not done within three days, the original giver may take back his charm.

The charms may be made from small scraps of material found around the craft shop. Small dolls, boats, birds, etc., can be cut from wood. Bright colors can be added by using beads or bits of yarn or ribbons for decorations. Children will enjoy creating their own charms, but those illustrated on the opposite page will get them started.

MINIATURE CHARMS

HAWAIIAN LEIS

The Hawaiian leis signify many things, all of which convey a message of special recognition. For instance, a man may present a lei to his sweetheart to express his love for her. A guest may receive a lei upon arrival or be presented with one of clove flowers as he departs. The clove flowers convey a special message of hope for a "speedy return." Often a neighbor will hang a lei around the neck of another upon bringing a message of good news.

Since leis are easily made and symbolize good comradeship, they make an excellent project for children in camps or playgrounds.

Spiral Lei (Fig. 1). This is the simplest to make. Cut four long strips of crepe paper 2″ wide. The leis are most effective if made from two colors, so cut two dark strips and two strips of a lighter color. Fold the strips in half the entire length of each strip. Fit the two dark strips between the folds of the two light strips. Fringe the edges by cutting them with scissors. Now string on a piece of cord, going around and around to make a spiral.

Circle Lei (Fig. 2). Cut small circles from crepe paper and pull the edges with the fingers to make a ruffly edge. String them on a piece of cord. Make several inches of one color circles, then make a section of another color. These may be alternated or many colors may be used. Many shades of one color may also be used.

Flower Lei (Fig. 3). Each island in the Hawaiians has its own lei of all its native flowers. A flower lei is made by using a heavy cord for the center. The cord is covered by sewing heads of flowers on four sides until it is completely hidden.

Camper's Lei. The lei at the bottom of the page is an adaptation for campers. Give a colored cord to each camper to start his lei. As a leaf is identified, it is added to his cord.

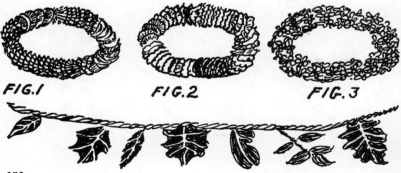

FIG.1   FIG.2   FIG.3

BAYBERRIES

Bayberry Candles. If you live in New England where bayberries grow, you will want the experience of making bayberry candles. Gather the berries in the fall of the year and place them in a large pot of water. Boil the berries until the wax floats on top of the water and set it aside to cool (Fig. 1). The wax will be a light greenish color and will retain the fragrance of the berries. Remove the hardened wax from the water and let it stand until the moisture on it has evaporated. When you have collected sufficient wax, re-melt it and put it into a tall jar for dipping the candles (Fig. 2).

Ironing Bag. Another use for bayberry wax is an ironing bag. Make a bag 6″ by 6″ from bright printed cloth. Place a cup of raw berries inside and sew the top together. When you iron, rub the hot iron over the bag and the wax in the berries will smooth the iron, besides giving the clothes the scent of bayberries (Fig. 3).

Bird Feeding Station. Bayberries make excellent food for birds in winter. Place them on a feeding board or pack them in small decorated bags and send them to your bird-loving friends.

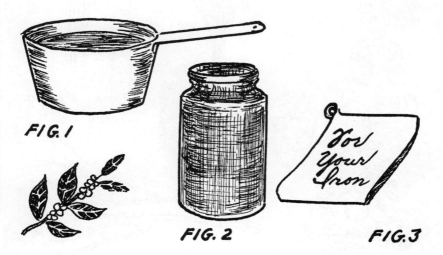

FIG. 1

FIG. 2

FIG. 3

SEED PODS

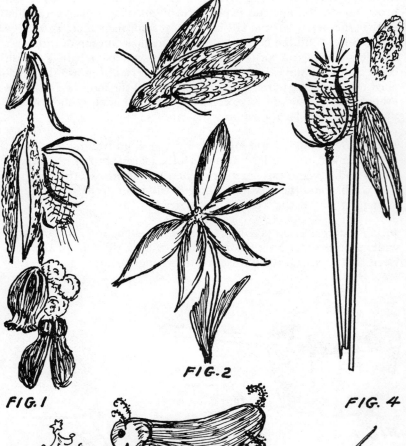

FIG. 1

FIG. 2

FIG. 3

FIG. 4

FIG. 5

FIG. 6

152

SEED PODS

Because of their many uses, gathering seed pods in the woods and fields in fall will pay off during the winter months. Pods can be found on trees, shrubs, or vines. Be sure to include all sizes in your collection. Keep in mind that pods must be carefully dried by hanging in an airy room before storing for the winter. This will insure natural shapes and prevent them from becoming mildewed. Also, if you plan to add color, the waxy surface must be removed—this can be done with alcohol. Sort the pods according to kind or size, and store in a dry place.

Since every locality yields different pods, we can only offer a few suggestions to get you started.

Charm String (Fig. 1). This is an excellent project for children. Learning the names of the many different kinds of pods is as important as adding color for decoration. After the pods are painted, string them on a center string, as shown in the illustration, and hang them in the kitchen or sun room.

Milkweed (Fig. 2). The milkweed produces the most popular of all pods. The closed pod is shaped like the body of a bird. After adding such features as wings, head, tail, and feet, it may be painted to resemble any bird within the size range.

Poinsettias can be made for Christmas decorations that will last throughout the season. Break the pod in half, paint the inside red, and arrange five pieces to resemble petals of a poinsettia. Wire in place on green foliage.

Animals (Fig. 3). Combine pods with pipe cleaners to make small animals for party favors. Let the imagination run riot and many new kinds of animals will be produced.

Pods for Flower Arrangement (Fig. 4). Wire pods to long sticks, as stems, in pleasing arrangements. Paint pods in various colors, and store them away for use in flower arrangements. They will add another color to flowers or give height to the arrangement.

Christmas Decorations. Bare branches make effective Christmas decorations when they are dipped in thin starch and sprinkled with mica flakes (Fig. 5). Color is added to the starch for variety. A large pine cone makes a Christmas tree when it is painted green, with white edges on the sections. A star at the tip, colored beads glued to the edges, and miniature packages at its base complete the tree. To make it stand, glue it to a wooden base (Fig. 6).

DEVICES FOR TEACHING NATURE

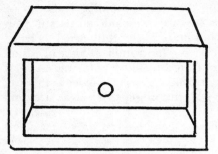

SLIDE

MAGIC LANTERN   FIG. 1

INSECT PUPPETS FIG. 3

STAR BOX FIG. 2   STAR LANTERN FIG. 4

GARDEN IN A BOTTLE   FIG. 5

DEVICES FOR TEACHING NATURE

Many devices can be used for teaching nature study to children. They also provide excellent program material for campfires. The following projects are suggested for use in a group rather than with an individual.

Magic Lantern (Fig. 1). Cut one side out of a large cardboard box, leaving about 1″ around the edges. Cut a piece of cardboard large enough to fill the opening, for the lantern slide. Cut a stencil for each silhouette of a flower or leaf. Cover the cutout with crepe paper in color to match the flower or object. Place a light in the box, so it will show through the slide.

Star Box (Fig. 2). On top of a hat box draw stars to form a constellation. Make the stars ½″ in diameter. Cut out the stars and remove them from holes. Place a flashlight in box. Cover with lid. The stars will be reflected on the ceiling.

Insect Puppets (Fig. 3). Make a stage by using three sides of a cardboard box, as shown in the illustration. Make the puppets from dried fruits and pipe cleaners.

Star Lantern (Fig. 4). Make a lantern from a tin can, and cut moon and stars for a decoration.

Garden in a Bottle (Fig. 5). Place some earth in a bottle, and lay it on one side. You can pass small plants through neck of the bottle by attaching them to end of a small wooden dowel. Add moisture with a spray gun.

One of the best methods for teaching nature in camp is to build a nature museum. The craftsman can contribute much to the project by making posters, building cages, making relief maps, models, and educational displays. Star charts can be made and tacked on the ceiling, placing the constellations in the general location in which they are found in the sky at nine o'clock each evening. Containers fashioned from lashed twigs and hanging baskets can be made for living plants. Other good projects are the making of terrariums and winter gardens.

Blueprint paper may be purchased from any store selling drafts-man supplies. It comes in a roll a yard wide, and you can buy any length you desire.

The only equipment needed is a printing frame—to hold the paper in place during exposure—and two containers for water, such as a bucket or dishpan. If you do not have a printing frame such as photographers use, it is possible to make one with very little effort. Take a pane of glass 5" by 7" (larger if desired); protect the edges by binding with a piece of portrait tape. Cut a piece of heavy cardboard the same size for the bottom of the frame. Secure two hinge-type clothespins, to clamp glass cover and cardboard together at the ends.

How to Make a Blueprint

Cut the blueprint paper into separate pieces the size of your frame. This must be done in a dark room or at night so that the paper is not exposed to sunlight. Place the pieces of paper in a large envelope *with coated side down*. This will enable you to remove a piece and place it in the frame right side down without exposing it to the sun.

Place the object you wish to print in place on the glass of the frame; then cover with a piece of blueprint paper, being sure the coated surface is next to the glass. Place the cardboard part of frame on top, and clamp the frame together. Now turn the frame over and allow it to remain face up in the sun several minutes. The paper will appear gray-green at first, but will gradually become blue. Remove paper from frame and place in a bucket of water. Wash the surface by rubbing with your hand, then place the print in a second bucket of water for rinsing. After the print is thoroughly rinsed, place it on several layers of newspaper to dry.

How Blueprints Can Be Used

Nature Prints (Fig. 1). Blueprints are most commonly used for making prints of leaves, ferns, flowers, and grasses. Such prints inspire children to compile notebooks in the various fields of nature.

Invitations (Fig. 2). Clever invitations can be made by using a flower, leaf, or a cutout paper design as a decoration. A rectangular piece of paper is placed near the center where the message is to be written. Since the light will not penetrate the paper during exposure, the rectangle will be white.

BLUEPRINTS

LEAF PRINT FIG. 1

INVITATION FIG. 2

You are
invited.

PAPER CUTOUT FIG. 3

SILHOUETTE FIG. 4

PHOTO PRINT FIG. 5

STAR CHART FIG. 6

Paper Cutouts (Fig. 3). Cut out paper silhouettes of butterflies, insects, or other objects and include them in your nature prints. Fairy-like figures should be cut from tissue paper; almost any story can be illustrated by drawing the characters and cutting them from the paper.

Silhouettes (Fig. 4). It is easy to draw a silhouette of a person on heavy paper. Cut it out carefully and place it on the glass of the frame. Cover with blueprint paper and expose to sunlight. If you make a pair of silhouettes, be sure they face each other.

Photo Prints (Fig. 5). Place a negative in the frame and cover it with blueprint paper instead of the regular photographic paper. Expose it to the sun several minutes, and wash in clear water. The result will be a blue picture with fairly good detail. Camp scenes make attractive greeting cards.

Star Charts (Fig. 6). Cut stars from black construction paper, using a train conductor's punch. Arrange the tiny stars on a piece of glass to form constellations. Cement in place with Duco cement. Once the constellations are arranged, any number of prints can be made, so that each camper has a copy for his notebook.

MESH WIRE AND LEAVES

OZALID PRINTS

Ozalid paper is a sensitized paper and may be purchased at any store selling draftsman supplies. The paper comes in a roll 36" wide, and it must be cut into pieces approximately 5" by 7". This must be done at night or in a dark room.

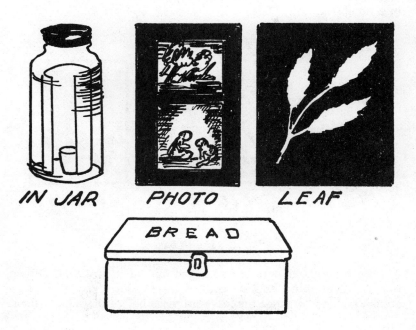

IN JAR   PHOTO   LEAF

BREAD

Ozalid prints are made similar to blueprints, with one exception —after the paper is exposed to the sun, it is developed in ammonia fumes instead of water. This may be done by covering the bottom of a Mason jar with household ammonia. Insert the exposed print, then screw the lid tight on the jar. A purple design will eventually appear on the ozalid paper.

A tin breadbox may also be used for developing a print. Place a saucer of ammonia on bottom of the box and arrange exposed paper around it. Keep lid of box closed until prints are developed.

CRAYON PRINTS

Did you make money when you were a child by placing a penny or nickel under a piece of paper and rubbing the surface with a lead pencil? A perfect picture of the coin appeared on the paper. Crayon leaf prints are made in the same manner. Select a leaf and place it, vein side up, on a table. Cover with a thin sheet of white paper and rub over it with a green crayon. You will have a replica of the leaf—even the tiny veins will show. Cut away the edges, and paste the leaf in a notebook.

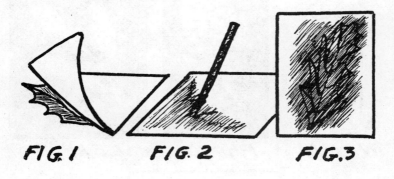

FIG. 1   FIG. 2   FIG. 3

WAXED LEAVES

Place some paraffin in a frying pan and melt it slowly. Dip in branches containing brightly colored leaves. Be sure that all parts are covered, and arrange the leaves in place before the wax hardens.

TWO PRIMITIVE LOOMS

Here are two primitive looms suitable for weaving in camp. Figure 1 shows the type of loom which Indians of the Southwest frequently used in rug making. Legend leads us to believe that Penelope probably used such a loom while waiting for Ulysses to return from the siege of Troy. It consists of a long stick, tied to the limb of a tree, and warp string suspended from it. Each string is free at the bottom and has a weight tied to the end to prevent tangling during the weaving. The warp strings are heavy string or cord. For camp, the warp may be strips of cloth, roving, jute, or even twisted ropes of coarse grass. The weaver usually stands while weaving. Start with a string two yards in length for the weft, fold it in half, and place the middle loop next to the first warp string on the left. Now bring the string around front and back, then cross on right of first warp string. Continue bringing the weft strings around each warp string, then crossing as shown in detail of Figure 1. When the row is completed, push the weaving up close to the stick. Weave back and forth in this manner until the mat is completed.

Figure 2 shows a loom used for making mats of bamboo strips, cattails, or grass. Drive half as many posts in the ground as you have warp threads. Place them approximately 6 feet from a tree. Now lash or otherwise fasten a crossbar to a tree trunk, as shown in the illustration. Tie as many warp strings to the bar as you desire. Bring every other string back taut and fasten to one of the posts. Use another stick for a crossbar and attach the other warp strings, allowing them to be the same length as those on the posts. The weaving is done by putting the front bar up, laying in material, and letting the bar down for the next row.

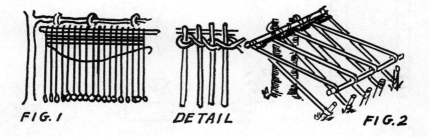

FIG. 1   DETAIL   FIG. 2

COMPASS

A compass is based on these facts: the earth is a great magnet, and a piece of metal can be magnetized by friction. Science teaches that the opposite poles will be attracted. Consequently, a point of metal will swing toward the north if it is the south pole of the metal.

Here is an easy way to make your own compass. Select a small square box, such as one that holds Christmas seals, and cut a round dial to fit the center. Make the dial of very thin cardboard or stiff drawing paper. Draw on all points of the compass with India ink.

Run a needle up through the bottom of box in the exact center and push through until the point reaches height of frame. Cut off part of needle that extends underneath the box. Now magnetize two needles by laying them across the ends of a magnet. Place the heads of the needles underneath the point marked North on the dial. Be sure to have them at equal distance on either side of North so they pull evenly.

Place the dial in box and suspend it on the point of needle in the center. The needle should be forced partially through the cardboard, to hold it in place. You might build a small wall of sealing wax around this place in order to keep the dial from falling off the needle.

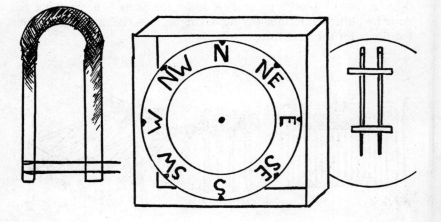

BAROMETERS

Barometers such as the ones illustrated are made from paper cutouts, with a piece of blue litmus paper included as part of the design. The litmus paper is made by dipping a piece of white blotting paper or cloth into a solution consisting of 4 ounces of water, 1 ounce of chloride of cobalt, ½ ounce of common salt, 75 grains of calcium chloride, and ¼ ounce of gum arabic. A chemist or druggist will make the mixture for you if you do not want to assemble the materials.

Figure 1 shows a child with a skirt made of the treated cloth, and paper cutouts for the other parts of the figure.

Figure 2 is a camp scene, with the treated paper making a blue sky.

Figure 3 is a calendar with a Dutch boy. The breeches are made of blue litmus paper or cloth.

These barometers work much better indoors, since they are very sensitive to dampness. In rainy weather the blue litmus turns pink.

A group of campers made up this little rhyme one day when they were making barometers:

> When the sun shines true,
> The sky is always blue;
> When the sky is pink,
> 'Twill rain, we think.

FIG. 1

FIG. 2

FIG. 3

CORN HUSKS

FIG. 1

CORN HUSK DOLLS

FIG. 2

FIG. 7

FIG. 8

FIG. 3 FIG. 4 FIG. 5 FIG. 6 FIG. 9

P.T.A. FIRST PRIZE

164

CORN HUSKS

Corn husks are one of the most versatile and accessible materials for home crafts. In rural communities they are usually plentiful at harvest time, and for those who live in urban surroundings the husks from green corn as it comes from the market are satisfactory when dried. A few of the many things for which husks are used are described here.

Lapel Decorations. One of the easiest of the corn husk crafts is the making of boy and girl characters from a single piece of husk (Fig. 1). Use the inside layers of husk, since they are softer and more easily handled. Dampen them by dipping in water and wrapping them in a paper towel. To make the girl, split one section of husk lengthwise and cut a piece 4″ long. Fold it crosswise and tie a cord around it a little below the fold, to form a head. Have the cord long enough to leave ends for hanging the doll on a coat or dress. The arms are a short piece of husk placed between the folded husk. Tie a cord below the arms to secure them and to form a waist. Draw features on the face with a colored pencil. To make a boy, follow these directions, and split the skirt to make legs. Tie cords at the ankles. These are used for lapel decorations or party favors.

Larger Dressed Dolls. The larger doll (Fig. 2) is more complicated to make but is a delightful toy or gift. Variations in dress and character are possible. To make a boy corresponding to the girl illustrated, cut the corn-silk hair, omit the skirt, and add felt trousers.

To make the doll, begin with six full-length sections of soft dampened husk. Corn silk is used for hair. Place the silk in the center with the husks around it, and tie a string about 1″ from the ends (Fig. 3). By turning this to the inside and tying another cord 1¼″ from the top, the head is formed (Fig. 4). The corn-silk hair is braided at the sides and bangs are cut above the face. The arms are made by braiding three corn husks into a strip. Tie at both ends for wrists. This piece is placed between the six husks which hang below the neck. Two of the six husks are turned up in front and two in back to make the skirt, and a cord is tied around the body to hold the skirt and arms in place and make a belt (Fig. 5). Three additional husks are tied to each of the remaining husks and braided, to make the legs (Fig. 6).

The cap, bag, belt, shoes, and hair bows are made of felt or other heavy material. The cap is made by cutting two circular pieces, which are stitched together at the outer edges. A hole is cut for the head, and cap is sewed to the head. The bag has a slender braided

CORN HUSKS

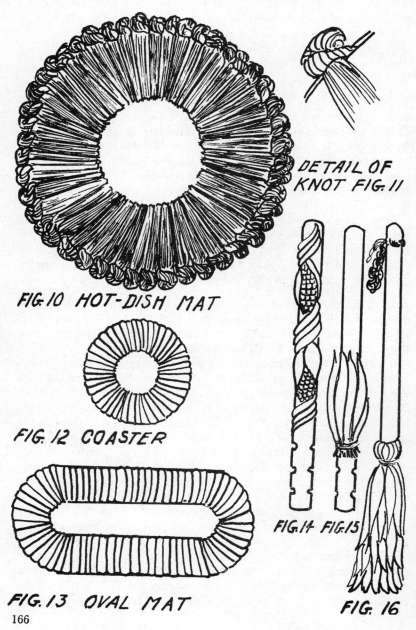

DETAIL OF
KNOT FIG. 11

FIG. 10 HOT-DISH MAT

FIG. 12 COASTER

FIG. 13 OVAL MAT

FIG. 14   FIG. 15

FIG. 16

corn-husk handle. The shoes are caps which fit over the ends of the legs. The jacket is cut from one piece.

A doll with a hoop skirt (Fig. 7) has corn-silk hair in braids sewed around the head. The arms may be straight husks tied at the wrists. The skirt is made of four, six, or eight strand braids sewed together, to make a cone-shaped figure which will stand alone. To braid (Fig. 8), use four, six, or eight husks. Start at right; place outside strand over second and under the next to center. Take outside left strand and bring it under the second strand and over next to center. Cross the center strands. Continue braiding from right to left, always going over the first right strand and under first strand on the left. Add husks as needed. To complete doll, put the husks hanging below the waist in the top of the cone and sew in place.

Hot-Dish Mat (Fig. 10). Make two 9" circular (or oval) cardboards with a 5" hole cut in the center of each. They are placed together and 1" strips of husk are used as the wrapping. Each strip is brought through the hole and the ends brought together at the outer edge of the cardboard, where a knot or twist is made. This knot is made by twisting the doubled ends toward the right hand and then making the twist into a tight loop (Fig. 11). The remaining ends of the husk are tucked between the two pieces of cardboard. The strips of husk overlap at the edge of the hole. Continue the wrapping until the cardboard is covered.

Small Coasters and Mats (Figs. 12 and 13). Cut a 4" circle (or an oval) from stiff cardboard. A 1½" hole is cut in the center of this circle. The husks are slit into ¼" strips. These are wrapped around the cardboard by passing the strips through the hole. The ends of the strips are tucked under as the strips are wrapped.

Broom. A useful hearth broom is made from corn husks. First, make a handle of wood. The top may be carved or plain. The lower end needs three notches cut around it 1" apart, with about ½" left at the bottom (Fig. 14). Select outside husks because they are stiffer and more durable. Turn the points of eight sections of husk toward the top of the handle and tie them in place around the handle at the first groove or notch (Fig. 15). Repeat this with eight more sections at the second groove, and also at the third. Turn this last group of husks over and tie them around the lower end of the handle with another cord. Do the same with the second set of husks and also the first ones you tied on. This completes the broom (Fig. 16).

BASKETRY

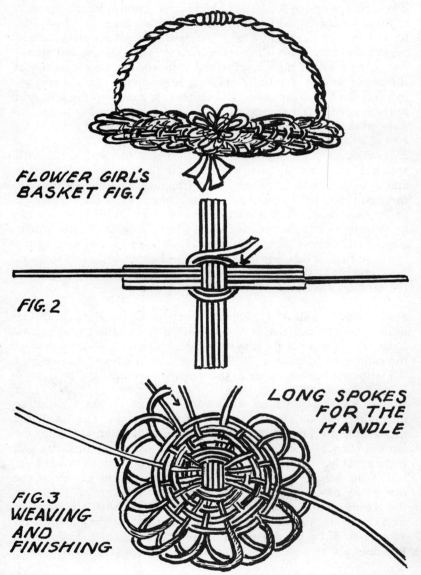

FLOWER GIRL'S
BASKET FIG. 1

FIG. 2

LONG SPOKES
FOR THE
HANDLE

FIG. 3
WEAVING
AND
FINISHING

168

BASKETRY

Baskets are made from a great variety of materials. Many of them grow along streams or in the fields in your own locality, and you can gather them yourself. Grasses of many kinds are suitable for sewed baskets because they are flexible and take dyes. Willow branches make durable baskets; they may be peeled or used with the bark remaining on them. Dried iris and corn husks also make durable baskets.

Baskets have numerous shapes and uses. Small sewed ones make containers for gifts of candy or cookies. Flat baskets are used for trays. Flat woven willow baskets might be carried by the flower girls at a wedding.

Flower Girl's Basket (Fig. 1). Use small willow branches with the bark removed. Soak the willow in water for several hours, even if it is green. Keep it very damp while working. Cut eight pieces for the spokes. Six of these are 16″ long and two are 28″ long. The two long ones form the handle but are woven in the basket. You will need one extra spoke which is 8″ long. Divide the spokes into two groups of four. Place them as shown in Figure 2. The extra spoke is placed beside one of the short ones. This makes an uneven number, which is necessary in weaving. Cut a piece of willow as long as possible for a weaver. Begin at the arrow (Fig. 2) and wrap the weaver around the four spokes, being sure that they are held securely. After two rounds, spread the spokes to form a circle and carry the weaver under one and over the next around and around the circle (Fig. 3). Be sure to keep the spokes flat. Always start with the thin end of the weaver. When the first weaver is all woven in but 1″, run the end down beside the nearest spoke. Taper this end with a knife so it fits smoothly. Take a new weaver and put the end down beside the end of the last weaver. Continue weaving until the woven area is 7″ in diameter. Since this is a flat basket, no sides need to be turned up. When the basket is big enough, end the weaving by running the weaver toward the center beside the nearest spoke. Be sure to taper the end. An ice pick helps to open the weaving so that the end can be inserted easily.

To finish the edge, run each of the spokes, excepting the two long ones, toward the center beside the second spoke from the one being turned. This makes a series of loops. Taper the ends as you did the others. To make the handle, twist the long spokes together and run the ends toward the center at the nearest spoke. Be sure that they are very damp.

For a natural finish on the basket, use clear shellac or wax. Colored enamel or radiator paint gives other finishes.

A Sewed Basket of Corn Husks. In making a sewed basket, there are several kinds of stitches which are satisfactory. The one shown here is the strongest. Commercial raffia, colored twine, or dampened strips of cat-o'-nine-tails may be used for the sewing. A tapestry needle or a very large darning needle is most suitable. The inner corn husks are used to make this basket. Begin by forming a firm coil of dampened corn husk, and cover it by sewing over it toward the center (Fig. 1). When the ring is completed, continue by enlarging. Use the figure-eight stitch (Fig. 2). When the bottom, or mat, is large enough, begin to sew the corn husks in rings one on top of the other (Fig. 3). For the cover, start as you did the bottom of the basket, and make this mat slightly larger. To make the side of the cover, do as you did for the basket. To finish the cover, make a ring of corn husk and sew it with a buttonhole stitch; sew the ring to the center of the lid.

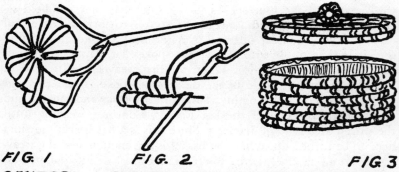

FIG. 1   FIG. 2   FIG 3
CENTER   FIGURE EIGHT   BASKET- COVER

BROOMCORN BROOM

Hearth brooms made from broomcorn straw are practical and make an appropriate addition to a fireplace.

First make a wooden handle with a knob on the lower end to hold the straw securely. The illustration shows a carved handle but it could be plain and painted. You will need about sixteen clusters of broomstraw, which is really broomcorn stalks. Assemble them around the knob on the handle and tie strings tightly at points indicated in Figure 2. Linen twine is best for this. Next wrap the tied space with colored raffia or twisted corn husks. Use the wrapping as shown in Figure 3. Figure 4 shows the broom completed with cord for hanging it on the wall.

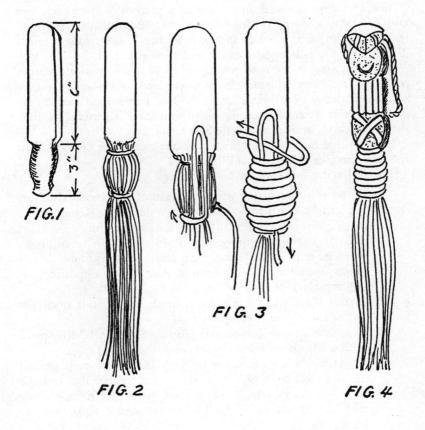

FIG.1

FIG. 2

FIG. 3

FIG. 4

WHITTLING

It is of prime importance that the blade of your knife be kept *sharp* all the time you are whittling. Accidental cuts are usually caused by putting too much pressure on the knife because a dull blade will not cut the wood.

In general, always cut with the edge of the blade *away* from you. If you must whittle toward yourself, keep the hand holding the wood behind the knife blade. Do not hold the wood against your diaphragm or your knee.

Almost any of the softer woods with a fine grain may be used. A good quality of pine is the best for beginners. It is easier to cut with the grain of the wood; therefore, plan so that as little cutting as possible is done against the grain.

The first step in whittling is to draft a pattern of the article you wish to make. Make a drawing of the front, side, and rear views and transfer to the wood block as shown in Figure 1. Keep your original drawings to use as templates as the whittling proceeds.

The best way to learn to whittle is to practice cuts on another piece of wood. You will soon learn to proceed continuously, taking small cuts and not cutting as far as the line in the figure at the beginning. Cut away the outside until you have a general outline, then begin adding details, a little at a time.

It is possible to hold your blade at many angles for cutting. This requires practice to become skillful.

The following hints might be helpful:

a. When you are cutting with the grain of the wood, withdraw the knife blade before the shaving is detached. Remove it by cutting *across* the grain at the bottom of the cut.

b. To cut a straight groove line, hold the blade at an angle, sharp edge pointing under line, and cut along right side of guide line. Turn object around and cut on opposite side, holding blade at same angle.

c. Always leave small appendages or delicate detail until the rest of the object is completed.

d. Very fine lines or features may be obtained by folding piece of fine sandpaper and rubbing with the folded edge.

e. As you approach the figure on your block, cut deep around the outline about $\frac{1}{16}''$ from the outside edge. Remove the outer wood by cutting away a small piece at a time; cutting with the grain, move the blade toward the *figure* on the block.

172

WHITTLING

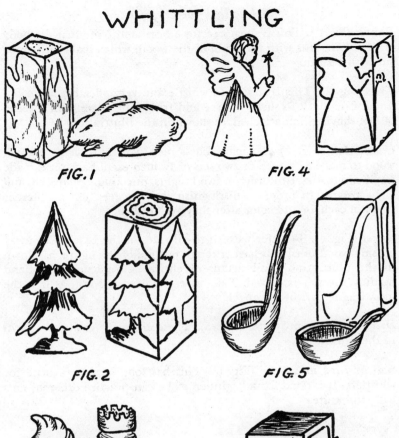

FIG. 1

FIG. 4

FIG. 2

FIG. 5

FIG. 3

FIG. 6

Directions for Objects

Rabbit (Fig. 1). This is suggested for a beginner. Note that the body of the figure goes with the grain of the wood, which makes it easy to cut with a knife.

Tree (Fig. 2). This is simple to whittle and very effective when finished. Cut block to shape of tree and fringe the edges with a series of fine shavings left attached, as shown in the illustration.

Chess Men (Fig. 3). To make chess men, you must have enough wood to make 32 pieces, or two sets of 16 men each. Each set is made up of two castles, two bishops, two knights, one king, one queen, and eight pawns. In order to distinguish the two sets, use a different wood in each, or add color after they are finished.

Angel (Fig. 4). Transfer pattern to all sides of the block. Cut away outside wood until you have a rough outline of the figure, as shown in the illustration. Add details of entire figure before the hand holding the star is carved. Take care of this detail last, as it is the most fragile part of the angel.

Drinking Cups or Spoons (Fig. 5). These are made easily, as shown in the illustration.

Ball or Bird in a Cage (Fig. 6). This has long been a favorite for whittlers. It is good for a beginner, as he can practice different cuts with the knife.

COPING SAW PROJECTS

These objects are cut from pine ½" thick. Trace the pattern on the wood, then fasten the wood to a table with a C clamp, and cut around the outline of figure with a coping saw. Smooth the edges and other rough places with sand paper, and decorate with poster colors or enamel. Shellac should be used over the poster paint. Features of felt may be added.

MERRY-GO-ROUND FIGURE

CLOWN PLANTER

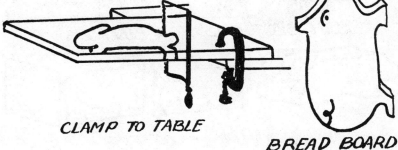

CLAMP TO TABLE

BREAD BOARD

CUTTING IDENTICAL PIECES OF WOOD

If you want to cut a number of wood pieces the same size and shape we suggest you use the following method.

Select a long piece of wood the thickness you need and sketch an outline of the article you wish to make at one end. Now shape the outside of the long edges according to the contour in your drawing. Cut the wood in sections with a saw, as shown in the illustration. This is an excellent method of making buttons, checker men, and animals for a Noah's Ark.

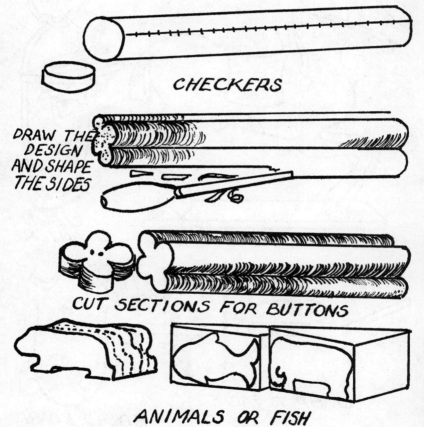

CHECKERS

DRAW THE DESIGN AND SHAPE THE SIDES

CUT SECTIONS FOR BUTTONS

ANIMALS OR FISH

POTATO PRINTS

Potato prints can be most effective if the design is carefully cut and stamped according to a plan. The prints are usually used on paper, since a water-bound paint must be used on potatoes.

Select a small potato and cut it in half. Be sure the knife blade is held perfectly perpendicular during the cutting as both sides must be exactly even in order to obtain a good print. Now draw a

FIG. 1

design on a piece of paper, and cut it out to fit the potato. Lay it in the center of the cut side of the potato. Incise the edges about ¼" deep with a small knife. Remove the background a bit at a time until the design stands in relief, as shown in Figure 1.

When the design is ready for printing, apply poster paint with a small brush. One or two colors may be used. Press the design down on the paper you wish to print and then lift it up straight, to prevent smearing the edges. Remember that all designs will be painted in the reverse. Letters or monograms must be drawn backward.

You will find many uses for these prints. We suggest that you use them to decorate wrapping paper, notebook covers, stationery, party napkins and luncheon sets.

PRIMITIVE UTENSILS

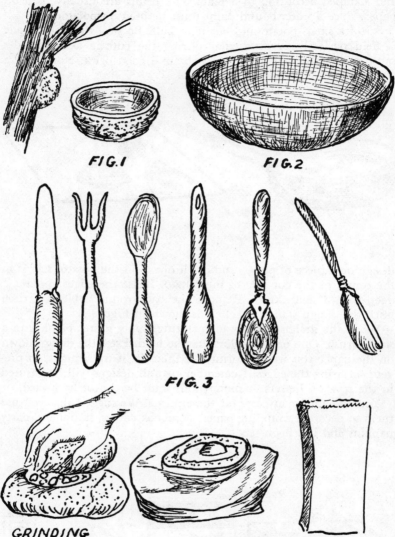

FIG.1   FIG.2

FIG. 3

GRINDING
MEAL   OUTDOOR COOKERY

PRIMITIVE UTENSILS

The making of primitive utensils is an excellent whittling project. The beginning of such a project is a trip to the woods in search of proper materials. If you are looking for burls, they are usually found high in a tree where limbs have been cut or broken away. A half-round bulge has formed, known as a burl. You must saw through it to remove it from the tree. Other materials are easier to find, but since much skill and labor is involved in shaping them, be sure to select the best.

Bowls and Drinking Cups (Fig. 1). These drinking cups and bowls are made from burls. The vessel will depend on the contour of the burl. With the burl fastened in a wood vise, gouge out the center a little at a time with sharp chisels. Try to make the walls as thin as possible, and smooth the inside with sandpaper. Add several coats of shellac, and rub down each time with steel wool.

Wooden Bowl (Fig. 2). We suggest you use hard wood for this. If you can find the trunk or a large limb from a fruit tree such as apple, pear, or cherry, it is excellent, due to the natural color. Cut out the general shape of bowl you desire with a saw. Do final shaping of the outside of bowl with a plane. Now turn the bowl over and gouge out the inside with chisels. It must be anchored with a vise of some kind, to insure safety.

Eating Utensils. Figure 3 suggests some which may be whittled from wood. It will take some searching to find wood in suggested shapes for the fork and spoon. The stirrer is a good project for a beginning whittler. We found spoons in an Indian Museum made by using a clamlike shell for the bowl.

Use of Stoves. Corn can be ground into meal by placing the kernels on a large flat rock. Use another large one for the grinder—one with a slightly rounded surface. Indians cooked on hot rocks. They were raked out of the hot coals from the fire, cleaned, and used for a frying pan. We suggest if you want to fry an egg you hollow out a piece of bread first, place it on the rock and break your egg in the center. This will keep it from sliding off the rock.

TIN CAN STOVE

This little stove is made from a No. 10 tin can. It has a hole about 2″ in diameter near the top which serves as an outlet for the smoke. On the opposite side at the bottom, cut a rectangular hole through which small sticks of wood can be pushed in to feed the fire.

Campers use these stoves on hikes. They are easily made and light to carry. Quick-burning twigs are used for fuel, and the cooking is done directly on the top. They are excellent for frying pancakes, French toast, potatoes, hamburgers, etc.

Plan to have a stove for every three campers. One person keeps the fire burning, the second cooks, while the third is eating. They rotate their positions until all are fed.

A large drum, similarly designed, may be used for making coffee or cocoa for the group.

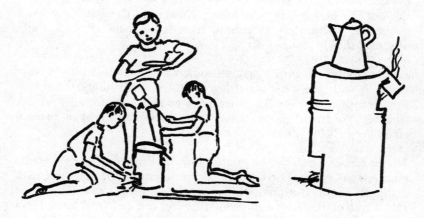

TWO CAMP COOKERS

Pressure Cooker. A coffee tin can be used as a pressure cooker in an open fire. This is an individual cooker, so each camper must bring his own. Place a pork chop or piece of thin beef on the bottom of the can and brown it on both sides; salt to taste. Now add any raw vegetable you wish around the meat; add more salt and enough water to cover the meat. Place the lid on the can and set it down in the hot coals to cook. A large rock in the center of the lid will prevent the steam from pushing it off the can. No dishes are required, as each camper can eat from his can.

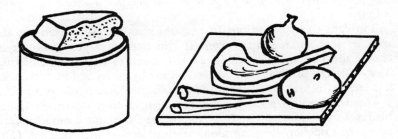

Corn Popper Cooker. This cooker is designed for small children who are likely to drop wieners and hamburgers from their sticks into the fire. A piece of tin is cut about 1″ larger than the bottom of a corn popper. Bend up the edges and fit it to the bottom of the popper. It is possible to fry almost anything in this; it is excellent for cooking in a fireplace as the fat will not drip into the fire.

Aluminum kitchen foil may be substituted for the tin bottom.

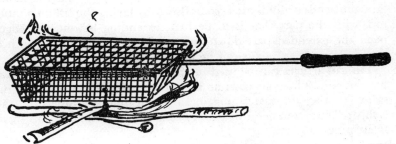

TIN COOKING EQUIPMENT

It is possible to make many useful kitchen accessories for outdoor cooking from tin cans. Note that we use the word "equipment" rather than "utensils," as it is not advisable to cook directly over a fire in a tin vessel. Although the tin will not melt while water is in the container, the solder might come apart and cause a leak.

Articles such as those illustrated on the opposite page are designed for temporary use, so easy, simple techniques are employed in their construction. As the camper has fun in designing and applying new uses for his creation, we suggest that each new group be allowed to make its own equipment. Since the craft costs nothing, it is worth while to make special equipment for overnight hikes and to discard the pieces after use unless someone has made an unusually good article.

Tin cans come in various shapes and sizes and you often get an idea by just looking them over. If you need a larger piece for a cookie sheet or another article, ask the camp to buy a sheet of tin. Try to design projects that can be shaped by turns or bends from a flat cutout; otherwise, you must use solder to attach the pieces.

You will need a good pair of tin snips, preferably with curved blades, to cut the tin. Carefully remove the top and bottom of can with a can opener, then cut along seam of can to open out flat. Cut a paper pattern of article you wish to make, and trace around it on the tin. Cut around the outline with the tin snips, being careful not to cut your fingers on sharp edges of tin. Now straighten and smooth the edges before the shaping begins. Do as much as possible with the snips, then use a file on other points. It is important to remove all sharp edges and slivers, to avoid being cut while cooking.

Clean the surface thoroughly before shaping the article. This is done by washing it first in soapy water and then rubbing the surface with fine steel wool. The shaping is done by bending the tin around a form and pounding in place with a wooden mallet. Round surfaces can be obtained by using dowel sticks or lead pipes for the mold. Straight bends or folds are accomplished by laying the tin on a table top, with the part that is to be bent extending beyond the edge; bend the extended part down and pound along the crease with a mallet. Various size nails can be used to make holes.

Tin can articles can be used in an outdoor kitchen or by individual campers. The craft costs no more than the price of a pair of tin snips. It also stimulates imagination and resourcefulness in the camper. We recommend that every camp include some of this work in its program.

TIN EQUIPMENT

REFLECTOR OVEN

FRYING PAN

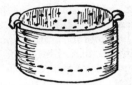

FRENCH FRYER

STRAINER

TOASTER

PITCHER

CUTTER & ROLLING PIN

LASHING

Lashing is a method by which two pieces of wood can be bound together with cord and remain securely in place. Lashing is a very useful craft for camps where out-of-door living is encouraged. The wood used will depend on what is available, the objects to be made, and what they will be used for. Twigs, strong saplings, or trees can be utilized. Both cord and string are practical for lashing, depending on the object to be made.

The clove hitch is used to start and complete lashings. Half hitches are also used, as well as square knots for ending the work. The illustration at the top of the page (Fig. 1) will show you how to tie the clove hitch.

Square Lashing (Fig. 1). Start with a clove hitch on the horizontal right. Work toward the left. Pass over the lower vertical, up and under the horizontal left, over the upper vertical, down and under the horizontal right. Repeat this procedure, winding several times, pulling tightly. Finish off by attaching the end of the binding cord to the starting end with a square knot. Or finish with two half hitches. Tuck the ends underneath the lashing.

Diagonal Lashing (Fig. 2). This is a method of holding two sticks together when they are crossed at the center. Begin by tying a clove hitch around the center of the two sticks. The lash is accomplished by making several turns around one fork, then the same number of turns around the other fork. Pull tightly. End as in the square lashing.

Telegraph Lashing (Fig. 3). This type of lashing is used for attaching cross pieces to a straight pole. It is possible to add one or more cross pieces if it suits your purpose. Select a long piece of string and double it at the center. Begin lashing by tying the middle of the cord to bottom of the pole with a clove hitch. Now cross the two strings on the upper side, then carry them underneath and cross again. Keep crossing the strings, first upper side and then underneath, until you reach the top of the pole. Insert cross piece under one of the crosses near the top, as shown in illustration. Tie the two ends together at the top with a square knot and make a long loop for hanging purposes.

How to Lash Two Poles (Fig. 4). This type of lashing is used for binding the ends of two poles or large sticks of wood together. This is done by tying a string to one pole and wrapping it around the two poles eight or ten times, arranging the loops so they fit tightly together. Tie the end of the string to inside log. Now make a separate wrapping several inches away near end of other pole. Cut a

184

TYPES OF LASHING

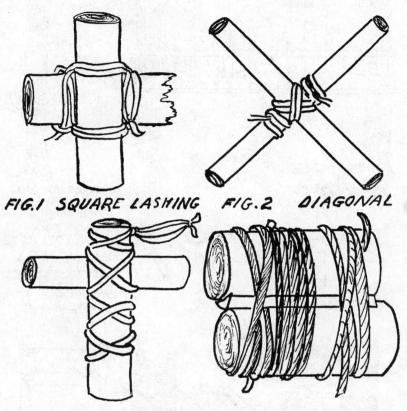

FIG. I SQUARE LASHING   FIG. 2 DIAGONAL

FIG. 3 TELEGRAPH   FIG.4 LARGE TREES

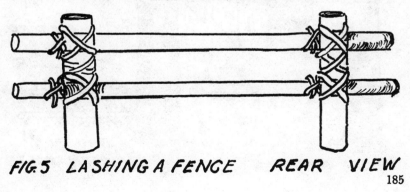

FIG. 5 LASHING A FENCE   REAR VIEW

LASHING PROJECTS

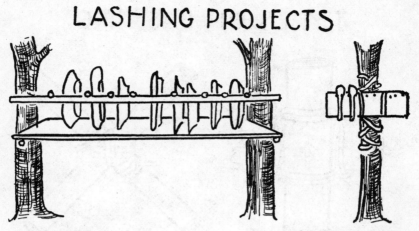

DISH RACK

SPOON HOLDER

COAT HANGER

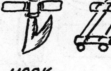

HOOK

SHOE OR SUIT-
CASE RACK

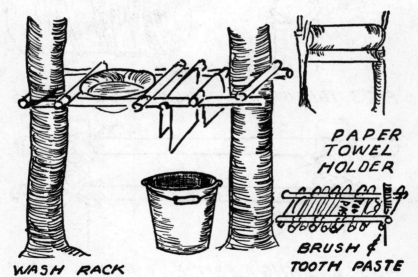

WASH RACK

PAPER
TOWEL
HOLDER

BRUSH &
TOOTH PASTE

piece of wood in a wedge shape and place it between the poles at point of first lashing. Drive it between the lashing to hold the poles securely in place.

Lashed Fence (Fig. 5). To make this type of fence, posts must be set into the ground several feet apart. Cut notches in back of each pole at point where cross pieces are to be lashed. Before cutting the notches, decide on the size of cross piece, as they must be cut the exact size. A double string is used for the lashing. Cut a long string and double it in half. Attach the center at the top of post with a clove hitch. Now cross the strings at the back and bring them down over the cross piece; insert the string in the notches. Bring the strings up again and continue lashing, as shown in the illustration.

Lashing Projects

Once you have learned to lash, there are many things you can make, especially for out-of-door camping. One of the challenges of living in the woods is to have as many conveniences as possible but to construct the equipment from things at hand. Lashing makes this possible. Here are a few suggestions:

Dish Rack. Lash two poles on either side of two trees. Fasten a board several inches below the poles to hold the dishes. Lash cross pieces 6″ apart to hold plates or pans.

Spoon Holder. This is one use for telegraph lashing. Drive small nails in the cross piece just far enough apart to hold a spoon. Knives and forks can be held in the same manner.

Coat Hanger and Hook. Select two sticks, one with a natural fork and the other smooth. The coat hanger will need a stick that is slightly curved. Trim the ends. Use square lashing at the joining points.

Racks and Holders. Other suggestions include a wash rack, shoe or suitcase rack, paper towel holder, and brush and tooth paste holders. Lashings are selected according to need.

Bulletin Boards. Two types are illustrated—one to hang and the other to set on a table. Cover the front with heavy cardboard.

Baskets and Covers. Small baskets have many uses in camp. The incinerator cover is easy to construct. For burning garbage, it is desirable to cover an incinerator pit with a mesh of green sticks. The green sticks will allow the refuse to dry out before it reaches the fire. Lash a strong frame that will fit around the pit, then lay the green sticks across each time the garbage is burned. A covering for a drain is made by lashing small sticks in a crisscross manner over a frame. Cover it with a small branch with leaves. The foliage will collect the soap or grease and can be replaced every day.

187

LASHING PROJECTS

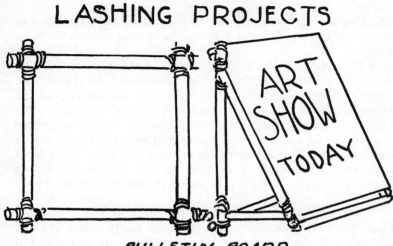

BULLETIN BOARD

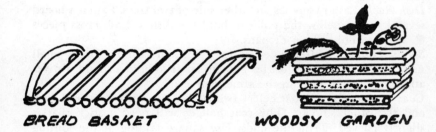

BREAD BASKET   **WOODSY GARDEN**

CAMP SANITATION

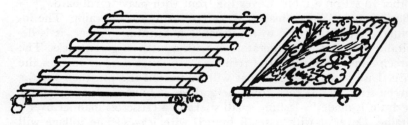

INCINERATOR   **DRAIN COVER**

CEMENT SCULPTURE

Sculpturing in cement is rarely done—probably because it is a messy job. However, if a studio is set up out of doors and you are suitably dressed, the results will more than compensate for your trouble. The techniques used in sculpturing cement are much the same as those in modeling clay: you must work over an armature, build up portions of your figure, and sculpture out the details of features. Cement sculpture is designed for outdoor use, so figures may be larger and workmanship more crude.

Since all figures must be made over an armature, or foundation, this must be your first consideration. Due to the heaviness of the medium, the foundation should be hollow in order to lend lightness to the figure. We suggest bottles of various sizes and shapes, jars, tin cans, or wooden frames. Build up the armature by wrapping with rags, and insert small pieces of wood for appendages as you go along. As a final layer, cover the whole surface with fine chicken wire or wire screening. This is necessary as it holds the cement and keeps it from sliding off.

You are now ready to mix the cement. Use a vessel for small quantities, or a wooden trough for large amounts. For regular cement use four parts of cement and two of sand; mix the dry ingredients well, then add enough water to give the consistency of modeling clay. You may make a special cement by adding marble dust to the cement instead of sand.

Cover the body of the armature with cement and sculpture it in shape with the hands. Allow it to partially dry, and then add the appendages. Add some water to the spot where new cement is to be joined and use thin cement or slip to seal it together. Now make the details of the features by adding a new layer of cement or cutting away with a chisel or nail. When the work is completed, smooth the surface with 00 sandpaper.

Cement is colored by applying a special paint for cement, which is sold at hardware stores. You may also harden and protect the surface with a coat of hard varnish. Sand it well with a very fine sandpaper.

The illustrations on the following page suggest garden figures— excellent objects for beginners.

CEMENT SCULPTURE

ARMATURE AND MATERIALS

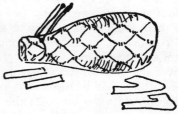

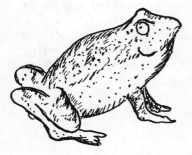

5

Crafts for Little Children

Certain underlying principles must be kept in mind when considering a craft which is to be offered to a small child. Since crafts require manual activity, the motor control of the child must be understood. His hands are not ready to hold small or complicated tools and materials. His span of interest is short; consequently, a craft must be finished quickly. Due to his limited experience, a complicated design will be confusing. The child's sense of values and tastes are being developed at this time, so what he makes should be worth while. All of this is a learning process in which he may develop a working knowledge of co-operation, responsibility, and creative ability.

Play equipment for young children is another problem. It is well known that a child frequently cherishes a tattered doll or improvised toy and disregards a new one after a short time. He will enjoy playthings which are made from blocks of wood, boxes, scraps of material, clothespins, paper, or almost anything of this nature. They need not be realistic—which is demonstrated by the child who attaches a string to a block of wood, calls it a wagon, and drags it around the yard.

Many of the playthings of this kind will require that the parent or teacher do at least part of the work, and thus co-operation is developed. Some equipment will have to be made entirely by an adult. Frequently the child can paint a toy and thus feel that he has a part in its construction.

After looking over the projects suggested in this book, a mother might want to start a rainy day box of materials from which toys can be made. Select a large box and store such items as cardboard boxes, scraps of lumber, clean wrapping paper, paper bags of all sizes, bits of yarn and string, scraps of felt, and empty spools. When a rainy day comes along, mother and child can fit the things together and create original toys.

191

SUSIE-BUR-RABBIT

192

SUSIE-BUR-RABBIT

Susie-Bur-Rabbit is one of the cherished toys of a little girl who has every kind of plaything. Perhaps she loves Susie best because she and her mother made her. It began when Janet's grandmother showed her how to fashion a little basket from dry burdock burs which they found at the edge of the yard when they were looking for the first crocus bloom. It was near Easter and Janet's mother suggested that they make a rabbit with the burs. They made a head, a body, and a tail by sticking the burs together. When this much was completed, they set it up and added hind legs. They forgot about the front legs. After adding more burs for ears, they covered the whole rabbit with a thin layer of white cotton. They glued pink paper eyes and a nose on the face.

"Do you know," said Janet, "one of my doll dresses would fit that rabbit if it had some arms." They attached more burs and covered them with cotton. When the organdy doll dress was found to fit just right, Janet was so excited she put a bow right between the rabbit's ears. "Now," said Janet, "she needs a name—and it is Susie-Bur-Rabbit."

Chickens are made on the same bur foundation, with small feathers for the covering. Pieces of red felt make the combs and wattles. Yellow felt makes the eyes. Dolls made of the burs are easily dressed. The hair is made of yarn, the faces and hands are covered with felt or suede, and the features are painted or appliquéd.

BUR BOUQUET WITH FELT FLOWERS

DRESSED BURDOCK BUR DOLLS

TWO GIFTS A CHILD CAN MAKE

Catnip Ball. Gather a bunch of catnip and break off the stems close to the roots. Select nine long stems, break off all the leaves, but not the flowers at the top. Tie the flowers together with a string and bend the stems back up over the flowers; tie stems with a ribbon (Fig. 1). Now take another stem, stripped of leaves and flowers, and—beginning at the bottom—weave it over and under the stems forming the ball. Since there is an uneven number of these, it is possible to weave continuously round and round. Add extra stems if one does not complete the weaving.

Pomander. Pomanders date back to the Victorian days when they were hung in wardrobes to give a spicy odor to the clothes. They are made by pushing whole cloves through the skin of an orange. First, select an orange; run a thread down through the center and back again to form a loop at the top. Tie a knot at the bottom, as shown in Figure 2. Now cover the surface completely with whole cloves, and allow the pomander to dry. Draw a gaily colored ribbon through loop at the top and tie a bow for hanging. If a child lacks strength in his fingers for pushing in the cloves, puncture the orange for him with an ice pick.

CAT NIP BALL FIG 1   POMANDER FIG. 2

CORN COB DOLLS

Corn cob dolls are familiar to every farm child—at least they used to be. Corn cobs provide an opportunity for a little girl to make her first doll. Simply give her a corn cob and select a doll dress that will fit over the cob. Fasten neck of dress 1½" below largest end of the cob, which makes the head. Add eyes and mouth with poster paint and sew some cornsilk on top for hair. Tiny pieces of cob may be tied in bottom of sleeves for hands.

Corn cobs can also provide entertainment for the older brothers and sisters. Kachina dolls can be made by adding color and features from colored construction paper, as illustrated below. Since cobs are red, they are excellent for making Indians. Just add paper feathers as a headdress, and dress them with cloth resembling buckskin. Insert the cob in a skirt of heavy gaily colored paper to make a peasant dress that will stand alone.

DOLL   KACHINA INDIAN   PEASANT

FLOWER DOLLS

ROSE BALLERINA

MORNING-GLORY

LILY

ROSE BUD

JACK-IN-THE-PULPIT

HOLLYHOCK

CHILD'S FLOWER GARDEN

This is a play device for a child who loves flowers and wants to learn about them. The garden is made by turning a cardboard box upside down and cutting rows of slits large enough to admit a splint or tongue depressor. Add a fence on each side cut from half circles of cardboard. To make it realistic, paint the box green and the fence white.

Flowers are drawn on heavy paper and colored with water color or crayons. Cut them from the paper and paste each one on the end of a splint or tongue depressor for a stem. They are then placed in the slits in the garden box. Suggest different arrangements for the flowers, such as placing a different color in each row, or flowers that grow near the water, or ones suitable for window boxes.

Flower pictures may be cut from a seed catalogue if the child is not inclined to make his own flowers.

PLAY STORE

Playing store is an excellent pastime for a rainy day. Cut two rectangular pieces of heavy cardboard and divide one at the center. Attach the smaller pieces to either end of the large one by pasting a muslin strip over the edges, as shown in the illustration. Paint the surface and draw parallel lines several inches apart to represent shelves. Now find several old magazines containing colored pictures of food. The game is to cut out the products and paste them on along the lines. After a grocery store is completed, suggest making a drug store, pantry for the home, and so on, if the child enjoys the project.

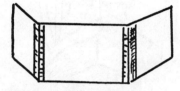 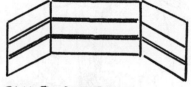

MUSLIN STRIPS   *PAINT SURFACE*

PICTURES OF FOOD
FROM MAGAZINES
SCISSORS
PASTE

PAPER BAG TOYS

FIG. 1

FIG. 2

FIG. 3

FIG. 4

PAPER BAG TOYS

Paper bag toys are excellent for rainy day entertainment for children. All that is needed is paper bags of various sizes, pins, strings, and colored construction paper. Poster paints or crayons may be used to add color.

We have by no means exhausted the ideas for paper bag toys but here are a few suggestions to start the project:

Walking Doll (Fig. 1). Three paper bags are required, two large ones and a smaller one about the size of a loaf of bread. The small one is used for the head of the doll. Add features cut from colored construction paper—hair, eyes, and a mouth. Cut off the bottom of one of the large bags and use it for the body or dress. Pull it together at the top and insert the head, then tie a string around it tightly to hold the two bags together. Cut arms and legs from the other large bag and pin them in place, as shown in the illustration. Tie two long strings on either side of the head. The child holds one in each hand as he walks the doll in front of him.

Animal Marionettes (Fig. 2). These simple marionettes are easily constructed from one or more paper bags. More action can be gained by using two bags for the body and joining them at the center. Attach a string at this point and the back can be lifted. Decorate the bags with poster paint or crayons.

Hand Puppets (Fig. 3). A child can easily manipulate a puppet made from two small paper bags. If necessary, split the skirt at the back so the hand can reach the head. Stuff the head with shredded newspaper, leaving space in the center for the forefinger. The thumb and little finger move the arms.

Paper Bag Heads (Fig. 4). Select a large paper bag that will fit over the head. Add features cut from colored construction paper. Since the headdress is used as a mask or in a play, the features should be emphasized in size or be grotesque. Be sure to cut holes for eyes. These heads are excellent for parties, as each person makes his own creation. They are also used extensively in camps for dramatizing animal stories.

CARTON DOLL HOUSE

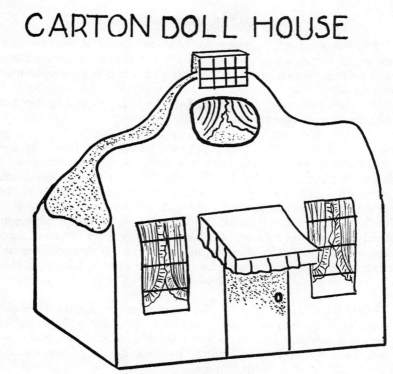

HOUSE

FURNITURE

DOLL HOUSE AND FURNITURE

A child will enjoy making a portable doll house from the carrier carton for soft drinks. It can be spread open at the top to admit furniture for the rooms, and best of all, it can be carried from place to place. Cut out spaces for two windows and a door on one side, and smooth the edges with sandpaper. Now add a coat of white paint and allow to dry. A red chimney may be added to top of handles if desired. The child might also like to add green shutters and an awning in front of the door.

The next step is to furnish the interior of the house. Paste clear cellophane over the windows and hang some curtains at the back. If the house is to be stationary, make an attic window by treating the openings of the handles in the same manner.

The child may use his own initiative in furnishing the room. Miniature furniture can be purchased at stores, but it is more fun to construct it from material at hand. It is surprising what can be made with match boxes, cardboard, pieces of wood and cloth.

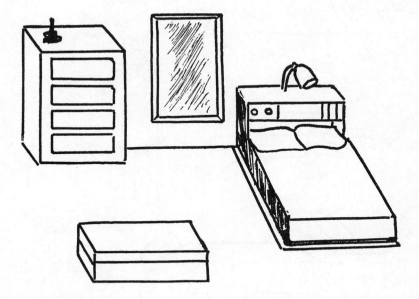

PAPER BOX TOYS

ALMOST ANY
BOX CAN BE-
COME A TOY
BY ADDING A
FEW FEATURES
WITH FELT

204

PAPER BOX TOYS

Toys made from paper boxes are just the thing to fill a young child's short-lived interest span. Every household has boxes of various sizes and shapes which can become foundations for an animal, wagon, truck, or train. With a little imagination they can be taken apart, cut to shape, and re-assembled. Features cut from colored paper or scraps of felt can be added, to make them more realistic.

To add interest, combine boxes with other materials. Drinking cups can be used for animal heads, as well as small pieces of wood, cardboard tubes, paper bags, and so forth. A piece of wire wrapped with string or paper makes a good tail. You will find the children will have more fun if buttons are used for eyes or broom straws for whiskers rather than making them with a paint brush.

There are several ways of sealing a box together again after it has been torn apart for shaping. The easiest method is to fit the edges together and seal with strips of gummed paper used for sealing packages. Another way is to cut muslin strips 1" wide, dip them in starch, and paste over the edges at points where there will be a strain. Sew together with needle and thread. To add color, use poster paints and a wide brush. We suggest the child be allowed to do his own painting. Crayons, of course, may also be used. If you want to dress the animals, just cut the costume from colored construction paper— this will add to the project. The figures can be made amusing, even the pig, by decorating with flowers or peasant designs.

If you use boxes that are covered with advertisements, you can paste paper towels over them. Make a starch paste and coat the box. While it is still wet, apply the paper towels and smooth out all wrinkles. Set aside to dry. Complete it with a coat of paint.

Paper boxes make excellent "pull toys" for very young children, and they need only a flat surface on the bottom to slide along the floor. When children are older, nothing but wheels will satisfy them. This can be accomplished by setting the toy on a wood platform for attaching wheels underneath. Large spools can be used for this purpose; run a long nail through the hole in the spool and drive it into the side of the platform. If you want to take the trouble, four casters such as are used on furniture can be attached to the wood.

In working on paper box toys, be sure to allow the child to do as much of the work as possible. He will accept the toy more readily if he has taken part in the actual work.

TOYS FROM LUMBERYARD SCRAPS

TOYS FROM LUMBERYARD SCRAPS

This is a most creative craft for young children. They may require some assistance from Dad to drill holes or pound a nail, but children can imagine things an adult never thought of.

To get started, make a visit to your lumberyard for odds and ends of lumber. If you can find a woodworker's shop, the scraps will have a more interesting shape. Soft wood is preferred, as it is easier to drill and thumb tacks can be pushed in to attach features of other material. However, bring the hard wood scraps along; they may provide a particular size or shape you want to use, and they also provide a contrast in color.

After the scraps are sorted, decide on a project. It is good training to go at it in a workman-like manner. The wood must be cleaned and well smoothed before beginning the construction. This a child can do with a piece of sandpaper. Fasten the sandpaper to a small block of wood so that it can be used without injuring the hands. After the wood is clean and smooth, the construction begins.

It may be necessary to remove bits of wood in order to complete a feature or fit it in place. Assemble the pieces in place and decide how they are to be attached. This is usually done by driving a nail up from the bottom or using glue, depending on the amount of strain. Drill any needed holes, and the toy is ready for decorations.

Since this is the child's own toy, he might be permitted to paint it with poster colors. This paint is suggested because the child can use it easily; otherwise, this type of paint is not recommended for decorating wood. However, we can suggest a colored finish that can be applied by young children which is pleasing in effect. Color the entire surface with crayons, then blend the markings together by rubbing lightly with a cloth dipped in machine oil. The oil dissolves the crayon enough to allow it to spread out and leave a waxy finish. Be sure the surface is well covered with the crayons.

Now it is time to add the features—and the fun begins. Ears, wings, and tails can be cut from scraps of felt or colored construction paper. Use broom straw for whiskers and buttons for eyes. This whole project is based on creative ability and imagination, so look around the house for anything you need to complete a figure.

PAPER MODELING

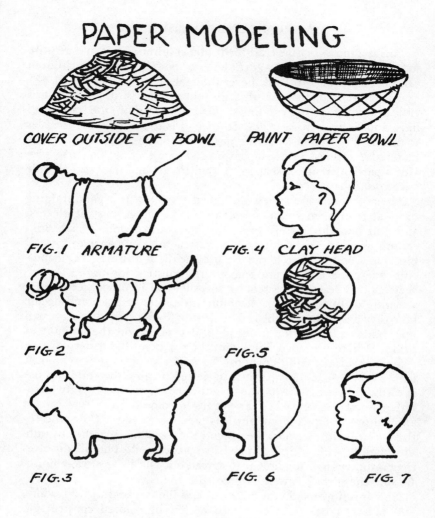

COVER OUTSIDE OF BOWL

PAINT PAPER BOWL

FIG. 1 ARMATURE

FIG. 4 CLAY HEAD

FIG. 2

FIG. 5

FIG. 3

FIG. 6

FIG. 7

FIG. 8

PAPER MODELING

Paper modeling is done by covering a foundation with several layers of paper dipped in starch and allowed to dry. Any kind of paper may be used, providing it is flexible as newsprint. Tear the paper into small pieces 2" or 3" in diameter so that it can be easily applied. Ordinary starch may be used for the dipping, but some prefer the wallpaper paste that can be purchased at a hardware store.

In order to understand how to model with this method, try making a bowl for your first project. Select a bowl from your cupboard and lay it bottom side up on a table. Rub petroleum jelly over the surface to prevent the paper from sticking. Cover the outside with a layer of small pieces of paper that have been dipped into the starch. Overlap them slightly; then add a second layer with a paper of a different kind, in order to keep all parts even. Add layers until the wall of bowl is the desired thickness. Set aside to dry, then remove paper shell from the bowl. Paint the entire bowl in a solid color, allow to dry, then add decorations. When the paint is perfectly dry, give the bowl two coats of shellac.

Papier-Mâché Animals. Animals are made by first shaping a wire armature to the form and dimensions of the body (Fig. 1). Begin building up the body by crushing pieces of newspaper and tying in place around the armature (Fig. 2). When the body has taken shape, apply small pieces of paper dipped in starch until the entire animal is covered. Add several layers, and use paper towels for the outside coat (Fig. 3). Features are added by either building up separate layers of the paper, or by using such materials as felt or oilcloth.

Heads and Figures. Form a head or figure from modeling clay (Fig. 4). Be sure to exaggerate the features (Fig. 5). Cover the surface with several layers of paper strips, and allow to dry. Now, cut the paper along the center of the figure and remove first the front and then the back from the clay (Fig. 6). Fit the two pieces together and join them by sealing together with small strips of paper (Fig. 7).

Paper strips are also used for covering surfaces, such as boxes printed with advertising. If an oatmeal box, for example, is to be used in a toy train, cover the outside with paper toweling, then apply some paint (Fig. 8).

Paper cups, boxes, or mailing tubes make excellent foundations for figures or animals. Check the illustrations for a few ideas.

USES FOR CRAYONS

FIG. 1

FIG. 2

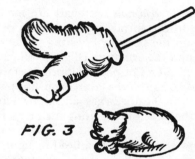

FIG. 3

FIG. 4

USES FOR CRAYONS

Here are four uses you may make of odds and ends of crayons. In fact, the results are so satisfying you may want to contribute a new box of crayons to the experiment.

Painting on Wood (Fig. 1). Wooden articles such as book ends or novel boxes can be beautifully decorated with melted crayons. Sketch a design on the wood. Select the colored crayons you plan to use, place them in small tin containers such as a muffin tin, and set the tin in a pan of water on a burner to melt the crayons. Since they must be melted while the painting is taking place, we suggest placing an electric bulb in a box and covering the top with wire screening for a stove that will keep the paint in a liquid form. Have a brush for each color.

Marble Paper (Fig. 2). Fill a flat pan with boiling water and shave thin slices of various colored crayons over the surface. As soon as the crayons are melted, submerge a sheet of plain paper in one end of the pan and draw it through the water underneath the spots of melted crayons. They will adhere to the paper as it is drawn through and form a marble-like design. These decorative papers can be used for covering boxes or book covers.

Covering Figurines (Fig. 3). Here is a way of preserving figures made from modeling clay by young children. In a deep container melt crayons of the color you want for the coating. Force a stick up through the body of the figure, to be used as a handle for dipping. Submerge the figure in the melted crayons for a second, then set aside to dry.

Crayon Etchings (Fig. 4). There are several ways of making crayon etchings. One is to cover a sheet of white paper with a light colored crayon. White, yellow, yellow green, or yellow orange are best. Cover this with a coat of India ink and let it dry. With a yellow or white pencil, make a drawing on the inked surface. Take a sharp instrument, such as a compass point or a pen, and scratch through the ink on the pencil lines to expose the crayon beneath.

Another way to use the ink over crayon is to make a bright flower drawing with crayon on a sheet of white paper. Apply the crayon as heavily as possible. Cover this with India ink and use a knife blade to scratch off enough of the ink to show the drawing. Leave enough ink to make heavy outlines and cross lines.

An easy way to make an etching is to cover a sheet of drawing paper with yellow or white crayon first. On top of this, put a coat of black crayon. Scratch a picture through the black crayon, exposing the light color beneath it.

PILLOW PUPPETS

These little puppets are made like paper dolls, only they have no arms. Cut a hole at the shoulders large enough to slip through the thumb and little finger, which become the arms and hands of the puppet. Use the top of a pillow or cushion for a stage. Since only the arms animate the puppet, they are used for making gestures, picking up objects, or pointing out directions. These puppets are especially useful in dramatizing nursery rhymes.

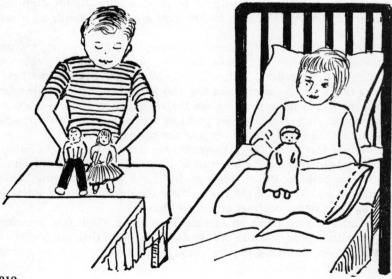

212

TOYS AND FAVORS FROM PAPER CUPS

PLAY EQUIPMENT FOR BACKYARD

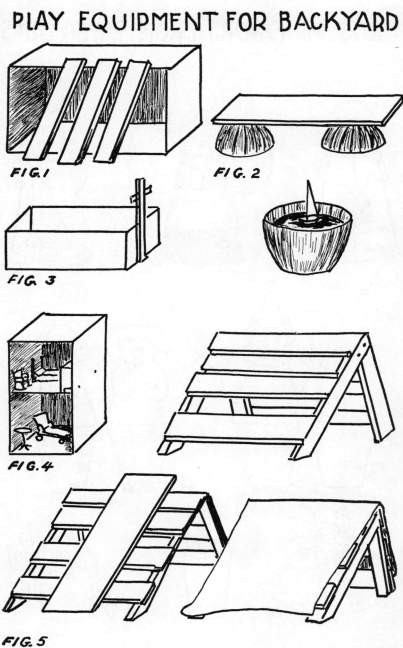

FIG. 1

FIG. 2

FIG. 3

FIG. 4

FIG. 5

214

PLAY EQUIPMENT FOR BACKYARD

Play equipment in the backyard is important for many reasons. It keeps the children out in the fresh air, builds up self-confidence, and strengthens muscles. Great care should be taken in constructing these articles as they must not come apart or break, and they must be free of safety hazards. They are designed for children to play with by themselves, without supervision.

A sandbox is good to build for a child's first play experience out of doors. It can be placed near the kitchen window so that Mother can see the child while she works. As the child grows older, a simple "jungle-gym" for climbing, a wooden pool, a swing, and other play equipment can be added. Here are a few simple pieces of equipment that require little skill to construct:

Large Packing Box (Fig. 1). Select a large wooden box, smooth the edges, and remove all protruding nails. Give it a coat of paint—if the child is large enough he can help with the painting. Also, cut a number of 4" boards in lengths to fit over the front, to make a cave for the youngster.

Wooden Kegs (Fig. 2). Find some small wooden kegs or wooden buckets and cut them in two. Sand the edges and paint the walls. They will serve as stools or as a foundation for a bridge. If watertight, they can be filled with water for sailing boats.

Box with Tongue (Fig 3). Put an upright tongue on front of a small wooden box. The crosspiece on the tongue should be the height of child's waist. Dragging this toy around the yard is fun—and it also builds muscles.

Doll House (Fig. 4). Set this doll house, made of an orange crate, up against side of the house. It can become a furnished house for a doll. The upper section can be made into a bedroom, and the lower part furnished as a living room.

Climbing Apparatus (Fig. 5). This type of climbing structure is excellent for children. They can climb over it without injuring themselves. It can also be used for sliding, by placing a short smooth board on one side. If it is covered with a blanket or canvas, it becomes a tent.

STANDING DOLL FROM NEWSPAPER

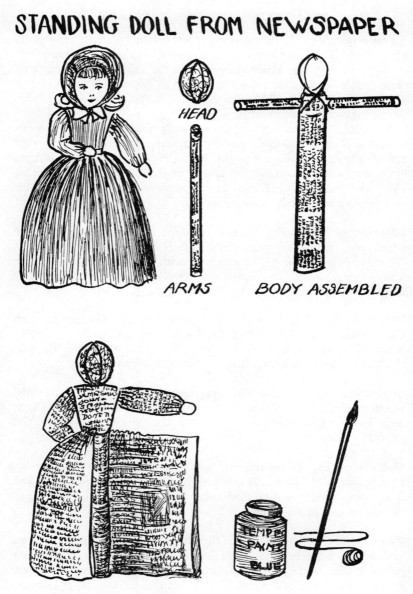

HEAD

ARMS

BODY ASSEMBLED

MAKING SKIRT

STANDING DOLL FROM NEWSPAPER

You will need two sheets of newspaper folded and rolled into a tube. Tie this roll or tube with string 2" from the top and 2" from the bottom. Make a smaller tube for the arms; one tube forms both arms. Cut a hole through the upper end of the large tube which is for the body. Slip the smaller tube through the hole and the arms are made. The head is a small bundle of dampened newspaper formed into an egg-shaped ball. Tie strings around it to keep it in shape. To fasten the head to the body, wind string around the head, cross it under the arms, and tie it around the "neck." This is shown in Figure 1. To dress the doll as a lady with a full skirt, fold newspaper double and dampen the open edges, which are gathered around the waist (Fig. 2). No sewing is needed. You just tie the gathers in place with a string. To make full sleeves, fold newspaper double, gather the edges after dampening, and tie at the shoulders and wrists. A waist is made of two strips of newspaper. The head is finished with paper hair and a paper bonnet and bow. Use tempera paint to paint the doll any desired color. To finish it, paint the features on the face.

The figures at the bottom of the page follow the same directions as for making the doll body. Costumes and coverings are also made of newspaper and painted.

CLOWN   LARGE BALL

WOODEN DOLLS

Wooden dolls made from a wedge-shaped block of wood are excellent for use in a nursery school or in the home. Select a block of wood 1" by 4" by 6". Draw an outline of a figure on the wood and cut around it with a jig saw. Now use a plane and shave away some of the thickness of the wood on both sides of the upper half, thus leaving an inch wide base so the figure can stand alone. Allow the child to paint on features and any costume he chooses. If crayons are used for adding color, rub over lightly with a cloth dipped in machine oil. This will blend the markings of the crayons and leave a waxed surface.

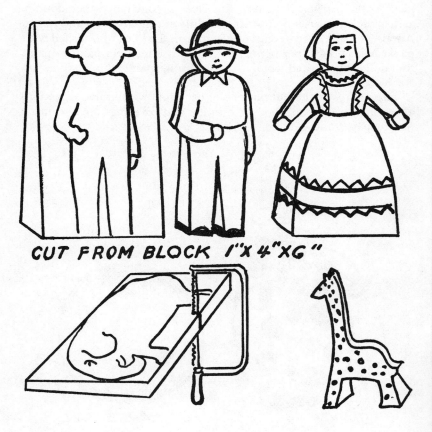

CUT FROM BLOCK 1"X 4"XG"

6

Crafts for Special Needs

The crafts suggested in this chapter are ones that many individuals will find useful, yet they do not fit into the other categories in the book. We would like to point out that there are only seven types of materials or mediums from which an object can be made—clay, wood, metal, leather, paper, textiles, or plastics. Throughout this book we have covered the beginning working techniques involved in manipulating these materials, so why not attempt to make some article that appeals to you!

Entertainment is an important function in the home. We have offered a number of suggestions for making decorations, posters, favors, and so on. They should be regarded as basic ideas that can be applied to any season or occasion. The success of this type of craft depends on the ability of the creator to improvise and to mold material at hand into colorful objects. The time spent on such projects should be held to a minimum.

The occupational therapist will find detailed directions for weaving on a four-harness loom. Weaving is an important phase of occupational therapy, and a large majority of the projects described in this book may be adapted for use in such a program. Suitable crafts can be found for all ages. Caning chairs is an excellent shop project.

Several of the crafts mentioned in this chapter can be utilized by an individual who wishes to make them for profit. Hand weaving has become an important home industry and a four-harness loom will afford sufficient variety in designs for the trade. Many hospital patients have found a ready market for such articles as greeting cards, table mats. Handkerchiefs decorated by the stenciling process may be sold in local gift shops. Finally, re-caning old chair seats might turn into a profitable business in any neighborhood.

MOBILES

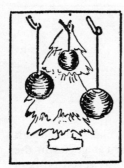

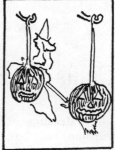

| GLASS BALLS | CORN EARS | JACK-O-LANTERNS |

POSTER IDEAS

THREE DIMENSIONAL   SPATTER PRINT

POSTER IDEAS

Here are a few poster techniques that may be adapted to any theme. In planning a poster, use a single idea and make your decoration accentuate that idea. Since a poster must attract "flash" reading, the contrast of colors is very important—keep in mind that dark on light stands out better than light on a dark background. Space is also an important factor—you have a limited area in which to convey a message and it must be well thought out before making a design. A crowded poster is not only confusing, but less attractive.

Since posters first of all must attract attention, the artist devises new methods and ideas. This is done by using bright colors, moving objects, three-dimensional or novel techniques. Here are several poster ideas that can be adapted to any season or occasion.

Use of Mobiles. Mobiles are moving objects hung in front of a poster to attract attention. They can be in any form, such as cutouts of bright objects, glistening objects, natural materials, or party favors. The ones suggested in the illustration show Christmas balls, ears of corn, and jack-o'-lanterns. They should be suspended on an inconspicuous string such as a silk thread or transparent cord. A permanent bulletin board might have two pegs extending from the top as a permanent fixture and painted to match the board. Whether or not they are in use is optional.

Three-Dimentional Posters. Objects that are in keeping with the theme can be sculptured from paper and superimposed on the design. Such posters are most effective and fun to make. Here are a few suggestions for the various seasons: (1) large valentine surrounded with lace (paper doilies) and ribbon; (2) red cherries attached to a painted branch; (3) a large red firecracker for Fourth of July; (4) dolls dressed in costumes. The ideas are inexhaustible—these are just to get you started.

Spatter Print Poster. Making a poster by cutting out designs and spattering the background with a contrasting color is easy to do and most effective. This is particularly effective in the fall. Pin leaves to a red or orange cardboard and spatter with black paint.

PARTY DECORATIONS

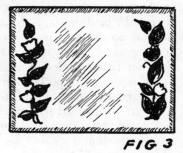

FIG. 1   FIG. 2   FIG 3

FIG. 4   FIG. 5   FIG. G

FIG. 7   FIG. 8

PARTY DECORATIONS

How to decorate is always a problem when preparing for a party. It is more fun to improvise and use materials at hand rather than go to the store and purchase favors. The suggestions illustrated on the opposite page are basic and may be applied to any theme or season.

Gold or Silver Dishes. You can make a room or table look elegant for a night by displaying gold or silver dishes. This effect is obtained by painting old glass dishes, candlesticks, or ash trays with radiator paint. You may gild as many objects as you like, even to painting monograms on the water glasses (Fig. 2). Broad, thick leaves such as rhododendron can also be gilded and they will not curl (Fig. 1). After the party is over, remove the paint by soaking the articles in a paint solvent.

Painting on Glass (Fig. 3). If you want to add some gay color to your room, floral designs can be painted on a mirror, window pane, and ash trays. This is accomplished by using a thick poster paint. If you have trouble making the paint stick to the surface, wash article with thick soap suds and allow to dry. Finger paint is also used on glass.

Candle Foundations. Set a candle in a flat holder to hold it erect, and decorate it according to the theme. The candle is used for a foundation and not for lighting purposes. Use a green candle to resemble the stem of a tulip or other flowers (Fig. 4). A large wooden bead is placed at the top of a white candle to form head of a Christmas angel. Add a halo and wings cut from gold paper (Fig. 5). The Christmas tree (Fig. 6) is made by cutting circles in graduated sizes from maline. Cut a hole in the center and string them up and down the candle. Cut the holes small enough so the circular pieces have to be forced in place. Add sequins for Christmas balls and sprinkle with artificial snow. Use any color maline you like.

Decorative Panel (Fig. 7). It is a good idea to have one large decoration as center of interest in a room. It should be placed opposite the entrance to give a pleasing effect to guests as they enter. A large frame covered with wrapping paper is good for a foundation. From colored construction paper make cutouts of any objects that fit the theme. Attach them to the panel with a stapling machine.

Bags for Party Equipment (Fig. 8). These bags are cut from heavy wrapping paper. Use a double sheet for each wall and sew the edges together with yarn, using a blanket stitch. Punch two holes on each side for attaching handles and reinforce them with gummed eyelet reinforcers such as are used on notebook paper. Fill the bag with party equipment, such as a pencil and paper for games, party favor napkins, and even a lunch.

223

TIN CHRISTMAS ORNAMENTS

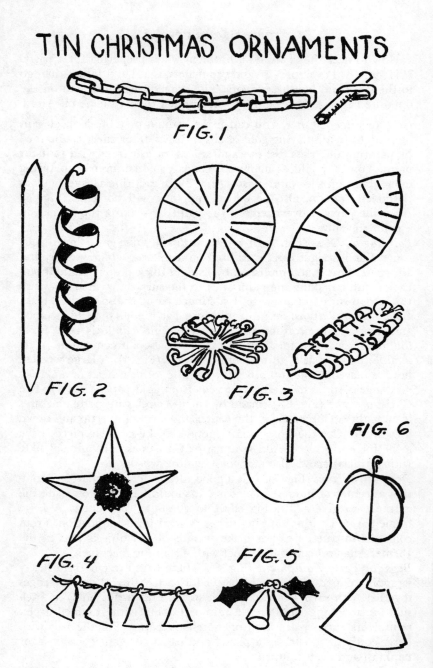

FIG. 1

FIG. 2

FIG. 3

FIG. 6

FIG. 4

FIG. 5

TIN CHRISTMAS ORNAMENTS

The making of tin ornaments for decorating the Christmas tree is an excellent project for a club or home. They cost nothing if tin cans are used and the only tool required is a pair of tin shears with curved blades. The tin should be cleaned with fine steel wool and the edges smoothed with a file and emery paper. Once the ornaments are made, they may be used year after year. The projects illustrated on the opposite page are simply to inspire your imagination—the number of articles that can be made are endless!

Directions for Making Ornaments

Chain (Fig. 1). Cut small rectangular pieces of tin for links of the size you want. Shape them over a round piece of wood such as a dowel. The ends need not be soldered together as there will be no strain or pull on the chain.

Icicles (Fig. 2). Cut pieces of tin ½" wide and as long as you wish for the icicles. Cut a point at each end as shown in the pattern. Hold one end with a pair of pliers and twist the tin to make the curves. Bend back the top to form a hook for attaching to branch of the tree.

Flower and Leaf (Fig. 3). To make a flower, cut a round piece of tin several inches in diameter. Cut lines about ¼" apart toward the center, resembling spokes of a wheel. Now bend the ends back toward the center as shown in the illustration. The same method is used to make a leaf ornament, except that the original piece of tin is cut in shape of a leaf.

Star (Fig. 4). Cut stars from tin and smooth edges with a file. Punch a small hole in center with a nail. Crease the tin from top of each star point down to the center. A sparkly glass button or earring is used for the center, the back of which goes through hole in the center of star for fastening. Color may be added by cutting a circle of red or green felt and placing it back of the center ornament.

Bell (Fig. 5). Bells in any size are easily cut from tin. Rows of small bells strung on red cord make attractive room decorations. If you have scrap felt in red and green, cut out a spray of holly and berries and cement on with Duco cement.

Christmas Balls (Fig. 6). Cut two circles of tin the same size and cut a ⅛" slot leading from edge to center of circle. Put the slotted circles together by sliding one slot into the other until they meet at the center. Use a small wire to attach to the tree.

CHRISTMAS TREE ORNAMENTS

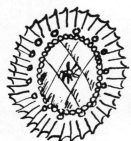
PIN WITH
FLUTING

EGG
SHELL

EGG SHELL

MIRROR & DOILY

BOTTLE CAP & DOILY

MINIATURE

PAPER
CUPS

PAPER
BIRD

CHRISTMAS TREE ORNAMENTS

Making your own Christmas tree ornaments is lots of fun whether it be with a group or in your own home. First, collect all the materials you think you will need, such as string, cement, cotton, paper, and cardboard. It is a good idea to have some metallic paper in different colors and lace doilies for backgrounds. Next, search the house for anything that shines or glistens, like small mirrors, tops from compacts, old costume jewelry, and shiny buttons. Here are several ornaments that can be adapted according to your materials:

A Pin with Fluting. Make a fluting of gold or silver paper and fasten to back of a breast pin from your jewelry box. The fluting is made by cutting a strip of paper 1" wide and making folds about 1/4" apart.

Ornaments from Eggs. Select white eggs to make these ornaments. Remove the center by punching a hole in each end and blowing on one end. Decorate them with small paper designs cut from red and green glossy paper. This is a Polish method of making ornaments.

Mirror Ornaments. Small pocket mirrors glisten and make beautiful ornaments. You may also use the tops from old compacts. Cut out a tiny scene from an old Christmas card and paste it on the front. Paste a small lacy border around the edge cut from a paper doily.

Bambino. Take a metal top from a soda water bottle and line it with silver foil. Make a tiny bambino and place it in the center. The body of the baby is made by rolling a piece of cloth and wrapping with two blue strips. Use a bead for a head and place a gold halo around the top. Place a small round lace doily at the back.

String of Bells. Very young children can make this decoration. String small waxed cups, such as those used for serving jam, on a double strand of red yarn. They resemble bells; small clappers may be added.

Miniature. This decoration should be made by a person who likes to work with miniatures. Use box top such as one from box of Christmas seals. Paint the inside of the box top as a background for the scene. You may own figures or cut them from old cards. Place them in a position to give a three-dimensional effect to the picture.

STRAW ANGEL

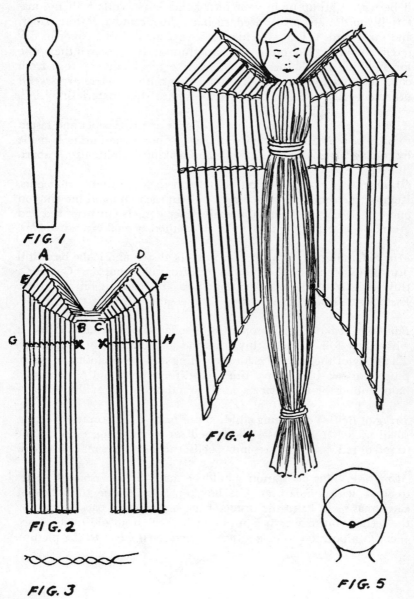

FIG. 1

FIG. 2

FIG. 3

FIG. 4

FIG. 5

STRAW ANGEL

One of Sweden's crafts which has been adopted wherever Christmas is celebrated is their use of straw for figures and animals. The reindeer and angels are most frequently used in America.

Wheat straw is gathered before it is harvested, to avoid damage to it. To make an angel, cut a head and body from soft wood. The head is 1" long and the body is 6" long (Fig. 1). Dampen the straw and cut twenty-five straws each 7½" long for covering the body. Flatten these at the thinnest end and lay them aside. Next, cut ten dampened straws each 18" long for the wings. Bend these and tie a string between the wings. Using the stitch shown in Figure 3, weave the straws together. (See Fig. 2.) Begin at A with two strings. Tie a knot and weave around each straw to B. Twist strings around middle to C and then weave again to D. Take another pair of strings. Begin at E and weave to B, twist around middle and weave from C to F. Take a third pair of strings, begin at G, weave across straws to middle and tie a knot at X. Begin at H weaving across the remaining straws and tie at the opposite X. Lay this aside and cover the body.

Arrange the twenty-five straws which you prepared first around the head with the heavy ends extending above. Allow ½" for tying at the neck. Turn them all down toward the feet. Be sure that the ends at the neck are flattened. Decide which is the back of the angel and place the wings under six straws at the back. Tie a string around all of the body straws just below B and C on the wings. The work will be firmer if you put some glue on the wooden body where the wings touch it. Tie a string around the body straws 1" from the lower end. Taper the wing straws with scissors. Figure 4 shows a complete angel.

A halo is made from a circle of fine copper wire and attached at the back of the head with a very small tack (Fig. 5). Use water colors to paint hair and features on the head.

Other straw figures may be made by following the directions given on page 165 for corn husk dolls. By following the directions for the sewed basket (page 170), wheat straw can be used to make a wastebasket. Six strands of dampened straw is used for the coils, and it is sewed with long grass or string.

229

TRICK CUTS IN PAPER

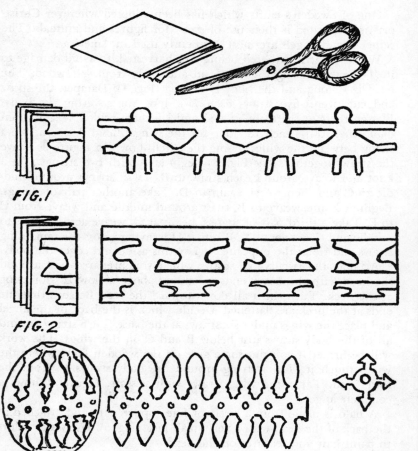

FIG. 1

FIG. 2

FIG. 3

FIG. 4

TRICK CUTS IN PAPER

Trick cuts in paper are very useful in a craft program, particularly if you are working with beginners. They are based on folds in the paper and repetition of design. By folding the paper different ways it is possible to produce designs in circles, triangles, hexagons, and so on.

The beginner can amuse himself by folding paper and making cuts at random. The results are sometimes astounding. As it is necessary to cut through several layers of paper simultaneously, one should use scissors with sharp, pointed blades. Also, the paper should be thin but sturdy. Glazed kindergarten paper is best for this purpose.

Explanation of Drawings

String of Figures (Fig. 1). Cut long strips of paper the width of height of figures. Make the first fold width of figure, then fold the rest of the paper back and forth to match the first fold. Be sure to add a ¼" strip on either side to join the figure. Cut around the outline and unfold. Features or decorations can be added with a paint brush.

Designs for Leather (Fig. 2). Trick cuts make successful all-over designs for leather tooling. They present an easier tooling problem than modeling around a realistic design. Keep in mind that space between the cuts must be lowered, so the outline of the design should be at least ¼" apart. These designs are successful on such articles as billfolds, belts, and purses.

Easter Eggs (Fig. 3). This technique is used by the Polish people to cover Easter eggs. They display great skill in cutting out intricate patterns in elaborate designs. Select a white egg and remove contents by puncturing both ends and blowing on one end. Use colored tissue paper or glazed kindergarten paper for the design. You may cut the outline of the paper first into shape to fit around an egg or an easier way is to fold a square and cut into it for a pattern, as shown in the illustration. In Poland, eggs decorated in this fashion are also used as Christmas tree ornaments.

Trick Cuts with a Design (Fig. 4). Fold a square piece of paper into four parts. Trace a design on one of the squares, as shown in the illustration. The design may radiate from either a corner or the center. Cut around the designed areas. These parts will drop out as you cut. Open the paper and you have an interesting design. Try folding the paper on the diagonal or in other ways for variations.

STRING OR CORD PICTURES

Designs and pictures made with cords strung across openings such as picture frames provide a means for using imagination and ingenuity. Small tacks on the back of the frame are used for attaching the cords. All kinds of thread, cord, and fine wire are suitable. A variety of colors, textures, and weights are used in the same design.

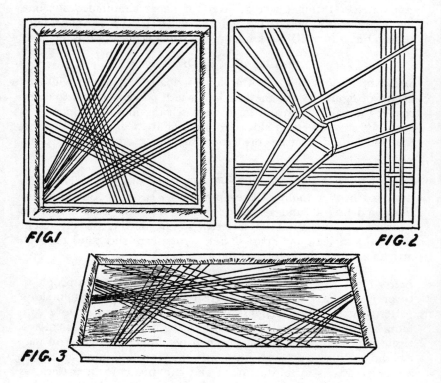

FIG.1

FIG.2

FIG.3

By arranging the cords as they cross at definite places, circular formations are made. Figures 1 and 2 will give some idea of the possible arrangements. The frames may be used without a background but dark cords will show better on a light background of paper, cloth, or metal. Light cords are emphasized by a dark surface behind them. A tray is made by putting glass in the frame and a background of wood to which paper or other material is attached (Fig. 3).

FINGER PAINTING

Finger painting, as we know it today, was originated in Rome by Ruth Faison Shaw, and her paints were brought to this country in the early 1930's. Finger painting is a technique anyone can learn and enjoy. It is now widely used in schools as an art medium and in hospitals as a therapeutic device.

Although you can really "make pictures" by this method—some of which you will doubtless view with pride and satisfaction—there is no long apprenticeship to serve before you acquire a technique. It is not just for those who have had preliminary art training. Indeed, if you have done any drawing or painting, forget about them for the time being, and do not try to carry over into this new medium what you have previously learned. Even though you may think that you have no talent for design or composition, if you putter with finger paints for an hour or two you will feel your imagination stirring and ideas will begin to come.

Commercial finger paints are sold in all arts and crafts shops and they can be ordered from art supply houses. But you can make your own, if you prefer. Mix wallpaper paste and water to the consistency of a smooth cream; add dry or moist poster paints. For adults the commercial paints will probably prove more pleasing. They come in a wide range of colors, which is an advantage if you have never learned to mix paints.

There is also a glazed paper on the market, especially prepared for finger painting. A beginner can use heavy wrapping paper for his first essays in this gay and happy-go-lucky art.

You will need a smooth, hard surface to work on—a table, or a tray or board if you are in bed.

The paints are soluble in water and however much you splash them about they will do no permanent damage, unless you are using a polished table for a working surface, in which case, cover it with oilcloth. If you are going to work in bed, roll up your sleeves and wear an apron or towel to protect your pajamas, and have someone spread an old sheet over the bedclothes.

First, wet the paper all over with a sponge, then smooth it out on the table. Rub out all the wrinkles and air bubbles with the palm of your hand, working from the center to the edges.

Put on several daubs of paint, according to the color you are going to use to start with, and cover the entire surface of the paper by rubbing the color over it with your hand. You are now ready to paint.

It is a good plan to work with only one color at first, preferably

233

a dark shade, so that the lines and markings will show more clearly. Work with your fingers, the ball of the thumb, the side of the palm, or even with your arm. If you use the tips of the fingers, be careful not to scratch the surface of the paper with your nails. Do not "sit tight" while you work but let your body "go" with your hands.

You might, at first, limit yourself to manipulation, to get the feeling of how to handle your paint. Repeating one motif over and over is a good way to do this. Study your picture when it is finished and see if it reminds you of anything. Perhaps by making a few changes here and there you might be able to find a subject or theme. If the lines run up or down, they could be worked into a clump of trees or a group of buildings.

The paints do not dry very quickly, so you can change your mind and rectify your mistakes. If you find you have made a mis-stroke, simply smooth it over and begin again. If the paint begins to dry, add a little water.

Later, when you have become adept and want to make finer lines than you can achieve with your fingers, use a pointed instrument, or a blunt needle. For a series of very small lines, try pressing a piece of frayed cloth into the paint.

After you have practiced all the tricks of manipulation you can think of, it is time to try a picture. The first one may come more by luck than by taking thought. If you haven't an immediate inspiration, don't sit and ponder, just make an imprint on the paint surface with your palm, a leaf, or a spray, or perhaps a geometric object, and see what you can develop from it. Make some bold tracery with your fingers here and there at random and then try to pull them together with a central idea.

Very soon you will want to paint in more than one color. The practice with finger paints is different than with water colors or oils. You do not mix your colors on a palette and apply them; you mix them right on your paper by putting one on top of the other. If several colors are used and repeatedly erased, they become muddy and lose their identity. To prevent this, cover the entire sheet with your over-all or predominant color and "mop up" spots where the other colors are to go. A face tissue or a paper towel comes in handy for this.

Perhaps you already have a picture in mind. You cannot sketch it on the paper first and then follow the outlines. So you make your sketch on a separate piece of paper and mark out areas on your paper indicating where the different colors are to go. Then refer to your sketch when drawing in the outlines of your picture.

By this time your artistic sense will have become sharpened even though you have never thought much about composition and design before. You will want to make pleasing pictures, with a sense of balance and colors that harmonize. There are a few fundamental laws of design which will help you to achieve good results in a very short time. The most important ones are these:

In finger painting, as with more serious work, you can get three-dimensional effects, particularly where one line crosses another, or if the paint is thick. When using several colors, there will be lines of blending colors where two colors meet.

In planning your design try to make the space areas pleasing. They must be in proportion to the size of the picture you are making, neither too large nor too small.

Rhythm is an important element in design. You can get the effect of movement by repetition and by changing sizes and shapes. For instance, if you have mountains in the background, lead up to them with foothills that become smaller in the foreground, or else graduate the size of your trees.

Proportion is another consideration. Everything in your picture should be properly related with respect to size and color. Colors, shapes, lights and darks, must also be harmonious. Without emphasis, your picture would be dull and lifeless. There should be one main center of interest. This can be accomplished by making the most important figure or object larger than the others or by grouping a number of smaller objects around it. By using stronger color in the main area, emphasis is also given.

Finally, your design must have balance; all lines should give the impression of leading toward the center of the picture rather than away from it. The weights of dark and light areas should be equal. If you use a color mass at one side of your picture, use the same color at another spot, in a different tone if you prefer.

TRAY DECORATIONS

Miniature Tree (Fig. 1). Fill a small paper drinking cup with plaster of Paris and insert a branch with small twigs in center before plaster is dry. Decorate the pot and add a small paper flower to tip of each twig. Paint the plaster green or brown to make it more realistic.

Flower Vase (Fig. 2). Use half an egg shell and decorate it both inside and out. Use a tinfoil milk bottle cap for a base. Fill the base with wet plaster of Paris, then set the egg shell in it. It will remain upright when plaster is dry.

Lady's Head (Fig. 3). Punch a hole in the top and bottom of an egg (make one hole larger). Force the contents of the egg out of the shell by blowing at one end. Fasten the egg to a cardboard base as described in Figure 2. Add features and headdress.

Snow Man (Fig. 4). Cement two ping-pong balls together by inserting a circle of heavy paper between. Add features and a hat.

Gumdrop Trees (Fig. 5). Insert branch in top of cupcake. Cut gumdrops in small pieces and fasten to ends of twigs.

Music Favor (Fig. 6). Bend pipe cleaners into shape of music clefs. Paint them black and attach to sides of a marshmallow.

FIG. 1   FIG. 2   FIG. 3

FIG. 4   FIG. 5   FIG. 6

236

SMALL FIGURES

These figures, used as favors, are dressed in costumes related to the theme. To make the body, insert a pipe cleaner into a soda straw and make an armature. The soda straw will make the body sturdy, yet it can be bent into any position you like. Use a large wooden bead for the head and add features with paint; unravel yellow or black yarn and arrange it for hair. Dress the dolls in costumes made of tissue paper or small pieces of cloth. If they are dressed in full skirts they will stand alone; otherwise, sew the figure to a cardboard base.

FIGURE   CHOIR BOY   FISHERMAN

THE LOOM

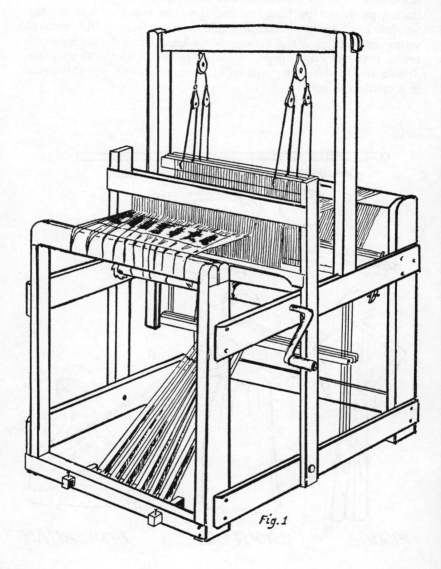

Fig. 1

WEAVING

Weaving has become so popular, both in homes and institutions, that we are including detailed instructions for weaving on a four-harness loom. There are numerous types of looms on the market today, but regardless of whether they are table or floor models, the basic principles in weaving are the same. Once you have mastered the technique of the loom you will want to learn how to weave with some of the exciting weaving materials that are available today. Explore the stores and shops to find unusual braids, cellophane silk cords, and so on, to add interest to your pattern. Even bamboo, raffia, and other straw materials are used for table mats. If you cannot find these items at your local stores, try the manufacturers. We suggest that you subscribe for one or more of the weaving magazines; they will furnish new patterns until you are able to develop your own.

The Four-Harness Loom

The four-harness loom is the one to be considered here. The ancient looms such as were a taken-for-granted article in the households of our forefathers were usually four-harness, and they allow for patterns of enough variety to be interesting without being too difficult. Figure 1 shows a simply constructed loom with four shafts or harnesses, and the different parts and their functions will be explained as we go on.

The table loom has two or more harnesses and is operated in just the same way as the floor loom, except that the latter is usually treadled with the feet.

There are many kinds of looms on the market, but whatever special features or labor-saving devices yours may have, the foundation principles and general outlines will be like the loom illustrated.

A loom is a frame for carrying and holding taut a series of long threads called *warp*, while loose threads wound on a shuttle and called *weft* or *woof* are passed backwards and forwards through them. The operation of the treadles or, it may be, a lever or another device, lifts up some of the warp threads while the others remain down, and this creates what is called a *shed*, a triangular passageway between the warp threads. Through this the shuttle passes, making a webbing, which becomes your fabric.

There is a craft jargon of weaving as of every other pursuit. A few words you have already learned from the foregoing. Now, study the illustrations of the loom and its principal parts and learn their names.

WARP

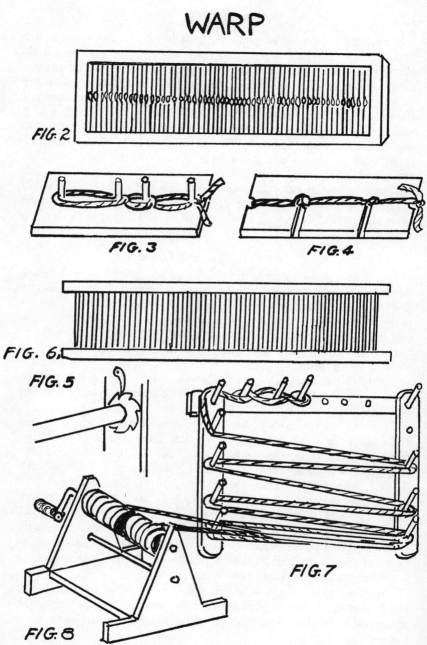

FIG. 2

FIG. 3

FIG. 4

FIG. 6.

FIG. 5

FIG. 7

FIG. 8

WARP

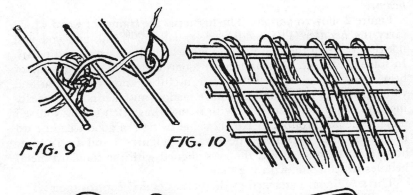

FIG. 9

FIG. 10

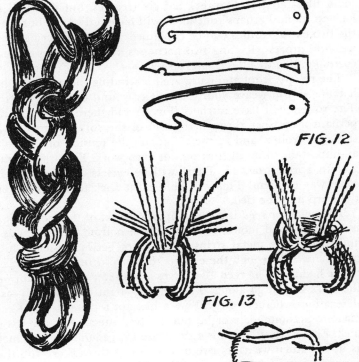

FIG. 12

FIG. 13

FIG. 11

FIG. 14 WEAVER'S KNOT

The flat bar across the front of the loom is called the *breast beam* or *front beam*. The one across the back, the *warp beam* or the *back beam*.

Figure 2 shows a *harness*. The harnesses are frames of wood which carry the *heddles*. The heddles are usually of metal, and you will notice the eye in the middle, through which the warp thread passes. In some of the old home-fashioned looms the heddles were made of heavy cord, waxed or varnished. It is useful to know that if you find yourself short a few heddles, or have made a mistake in your threading, you can make extra ones with string, thus often saving yourself much time and trouble. A No. 12 seine twine is a good weight cord to use for these improvised heddles and Figures 3 and 4 will show how to get them accurate, the eyes aligned with the standard metal heddles which come with the looms.

The *treadles* are attached to the harnesses and control them. The loom illustrated in Figure 1 has six treadles, but it is still a four-harness loom. Perhaps your loom will have only four, but the use of the two extra treadles will be explained when we describe the actual weaving process. Raising two harnesses at once by depressing their corresponding treadles creates a shed.

The rollers, front and back, are for winding the warp and holding it taut. As you weave your cloth, it is wound onto the front roller. The rollers will have ratchets (Fig. 5) and there will be a crank or perhaps a crossbar through the end of the roller to make winding easy. The rollers and ratchets regulate the tension of the warp, the all-important thing in turning out even work. Each roller will have a cloth apron attached. There will be eyelets and tape fastened in some way to them. This will hold a flat stick to which the ends of the warp must be tied.

The *comb* or *reed* is a very important part of the loom (Fig. 6). It is, in most hand looms, attached at the bottom, and it moves back and forth. The metal strips have spaces between them which are called *dents*. Through these dents the warp thread passes on its way to the heddles. The reed also serves as a *beater* or *batten* for *beating* the work as you go along. The beating—lightly or strongly—is what determines whether you will get a loose or a close weave. Reeds are made to accommodate eight, ten, twelve, fifteen, etc., threads to the inch. Fifteen to the inch is a good size for general work. Sometimes, as in fine linen weaving, two or even three threads are run through every dent and from two to four dents at each end are always threaded double to make a selvedge. If you are using a thick-ply woolen warp you will need a coarser reed, but the fifteen-to-the-inch size will take

242

two-ply or three-ply wool and it is practical for carpet warp and the moderately fine threads.

Any type of shuttle can be used.

Some looms come from the manufacturers already set up; others are collapsible and will be delivered in parts. However, instructions for setting them up always come with them, and many manufacturers will also send books of directions and drafts of patterns. It is wise to buy a loom wide enough to make rugs or lengths of drapery, for you can make narrower widths on it, such as table runners and luncheon doilies. You will find that getting familiar with your loom and feeling at home with it does not take long.

Preparing a loom for weaving is called *dressing the loom*. Putting on the warp is called *beaming*. The first step towards this is *making the warp*. There are looms which come with an attachment for making warp. If you do a great deal of weaving and use long warps, you can have them wound at some of the mills, ready to put on the loom. However, you must know how to make a warp yourself, to qualify as a weaver.

Figure 7 shows a *warping frame* for hanging on the wall. You can get or make them in various sizes—two and one-half, five, eight, ten, and twelve-yard lengths, and longer if you desire. Eight or ten yards is a good length warp and more economical than the shorter lengths. There must always be an allowance of about half a yard for "tying on."

The *spool frame* (shown feeding the warping frame in Figure 8) is a great convenience. For a wide pattern calling for several hundred threads, you can put four or six spools on a frame and by tying the ends of thread together warp four at a time, thus lessening the work considerably. For example, if you require 100 warp threads and put four spools on your frame, you will have to go round it only twenty-five times instead of one hundred times.

You will see in the illustration of the warping frame that there is a place where the threads cross in such a way as to make a definite opening. This is called the "lease" or "cross," and it is all-important, for without it the warp would be useless. By studying Figure 9 and Figure 10 you will see why this is so. The *lease sticks,* which go through the lease, separate the threads into even sections, keeping some up and some down. The lease sticks are also called *shed sticks,* for they make the *tabby sheds.* To doubly insure that you will not lose the lease or cross in the warp, tie pieces of colored thread through the lease, one on each side of the opening.

Now *crochet* your warp (Fig. 11) as you remove it from the frame. You do exactly as you would in making a chain stitch with a crochet

243

needle: Make a loop, using your right hand, and pull the "bout" of warp threads through it, making another loop, and so on. This is to prevent tangling. Tangled warp is the bane of a weaver's life, so handle it with the greatest care. If you are going to weave a narrow strip, like a scarf, you can make your warp all in one chain, but if you are planning a wide strip with several hundred threads, you will have to make several chains.

Suppose that you are going to use three hundred warp threads. A good way to do would be to use four spools of warp. Tie the ends together. Attach it to the starting peg. Study the illustration. It is easy to follow the route of the warp from the picture. You will make three chains of a hundred threads each, perhaps. To do this you would have to go round your frame twenty-five times with each series of four threads. (It might be more convenient to make six chains of fifty threads, depending upon the ply of your warp.) Do not cut your warp, but tie a string at each end, as well as the two ties to mark the lease.

The next step is to fasten the warp onto the beam of your loom. This, as we mentioned before, is called *beaming*. The loom can be threaded from the front or from the back, and many experienced weavers prefer the back-to-front method. But it is easier for most beginners to understand the importance of certain points by first learning to thread from the front. After you have done this once, you can thread from the back if you like, because then you will know the what and why of every operation. In other words, when you have fully mastered the principles, small details will be a matter of individual technique.

Always warp a few extra lengths of thread, in case you lose or break one or make a mistake.

Now that you have learned about your loom and its appurtenances and the preparations for weaving, let us set up a table loom and make a woolen scarf.

We will use a loom with only two harnesses, and so it will make only a tabby weave. The variations in your scarf, therefore, must come from color.

Tabby is plain weaving, one thread over and one thread under, like darning, and it is the foundation of your cloth, for its serves as the binder. It is customary in the more usual types of weaving to use a shot of tabby after every pattern shot. When you are doing pattern weaving there will be "skips" where the pattern is overshot, and without the firm tabby weaving in between these overshots your fabric would lack body.

There are many ways of getting interesting effects with your two-

244

harness weaving. You can have colored borders, or some colored warp threads to contrast with the predominant warp color. Checks result from stripes of colored warp crossed by contrasting weft. You can also have ridges by threading a number of dents double at certain intervals. We will suppose that, this first time, you have chosen white warp with maroon and aquamarine stripes at the ends. The scarf is to be two yards long and twelve inches wide. Your reed has fifteen dents to the inch. You will therefore need 180 warp threads. For this you will use a hard twisted wool, and a softer wool of slightly thicker ply, if you like, for the weft. About two-ply would be right for the warp.

Make your warp and weft into balls, just as for knitting, and handle it carefully, without pulling, which weakens it. Put your warp balls into a box on the floor, for the spool frame can be used only for thread which comes on tubes. Then proceed as described before to make your warp and to chain it.

Take your lease sticks and put them through the cross or lease and tie the sticks securely to the front beam of your loom. Suppose you have an eighteen-inch loom. Your scarf is to be twelve inches, so that will mean that you will begin threading your dents three inches from the right end.

Figure 12 shows three types of hooks for taking the threads through the dents and heddles, or *entering* your warp.

But first, when the lease sticks have been firmly tied to the front beam and the threads spread out as in Figure 10, you cut the forward ends. Leave the lease sticks in, however. Now, start passing the threads through the dents, being sure not to miss a single one, for this would spoil your whole scarf, leaving what would appear to be a drawn thread throughout the length. This can be done for the sake of design, but that will come later. You must also be careful not to cross the threads. The function of the lease and the lease sticks is to prevent this crossing of threads, which would make weaving impossible.

Through the first dent, three inches from the right end of your breast beam, enter two threads. Also through the next one. (You have allowed for this by measuring off 184 threads instead of 180 threads—the four extra ones for the selvedge and a few more "just in case.") After the second dent, pass one thread through each dent until you have reached the point three inches from the left side (making sure to thread for the selvedge at this end, too). Now, check over your work carefully, and see that you have no empty dents and no crossed threads. After your first experience in weaving, you will understand why we keep repeating certain points.

As this is to be a plain weave, or tabby, you will not need a threading draft. We will study drafts later when we come to pattern weaving. For the scarf, the procedure is to put the first two threads through the first back heddle, the next two through the first front heddle. You have now threaded for the selvedge. Continue with single threads first in a back heddle, and then in a front heddle until all your threads have been entered. It is good practice to tie the warp threads up behind the heddles in groups, so that they won't slip out. In this case, tie them in groups of fifteen (seventeen for the selvedge ends) and that will make it easy to check them. Checking dents and heddles carefully is absolutely necessary. Preparing the loom is very particular work, but it is so varied that it never becomes dull. However, having to undo and do all over again is tedious and a strain on patience, so work slowly, and check as you go.

If you can press someone into service to help in checking and also in tying onto the back roller, it will simplify the process for you. You can do it all alone in a pinch, but it is easier and considerably quicker with a helper.

The warp is now ready to be tied onto the back roller. It will go over the warp beam, and the apron with the stick taped to it must be raised in the back to meet it. Over the stick and between the tapes, tie a group of warp threads. The loop knot used for this is illustrated in Figure 13. This is a crucial moment, for the tension and evenness of the warp will determine the quality of your work. Begin tying in the middle and work from one side to the other until you reach the ends. The ends have a tendency to sag and this you must watch. You will need a length of brown paper an inch or so wider than your weaving to hold the warp threads in their proper places when you begin to roll.

There are some looms which have the back roller divided with pegs or in some other way so that the groups of warp threads will be separated. If your loom has these roller divisions you will not need the paper. Some looms are constructed to take round bobbins of warp thread. Any such variations, however, will not alter the principles and the basic procedure.

If everything is in order, you can now begin to wind your warp onto the back roller. This will entail *combing* the warp with your fingers to straighten it out as you wind. Someone must hold the warp in front and help at this stage. The warp threads must be held in two groups at equal tension or they will not wind straight and even, as they should. The combing is done by the person in front, so that the threads will go smoothly through the heddles. When the chain ends have been wound up near to the breast beam it is time to tie

246

the front ends to the front roller apron, exactly as you did in the back. Cut the ends carefully now, but be sure not to lose your shed sticks. Leave them in their places. Make another check. If you have made a good job of it, you will not have to re-roll. If the threads in front of the heddles by the breast beam are held taut in two equal groups by a helper while the warp is being wound slowly and carefully onto the back roller, all should be well, and you can get your proper tension by the use of the ratchets. Then you can start weaving. A good way to test the tension is to brush your hand lightly over the taut warp and if there is just a tiny "give" and it goes right back, it is at correct tension. Be sure that the ends are as tight as the middle, or you will have a poor, wavy edge.

In large weaving it is usual to begin with a few shots of "roving" or of carpet rags, which can be pulled out when you have finished your strip. This makes a solid piece against which to beat the body of your work when you begin. However, you will have a fringe on your scarf, so just start with your white weft, which you should have wound onto the shuttle, and you can pull out the first few rows when your scarf is finished.

The table loom may operate with levers. Whatever the device, press the one on the right hand (weaving is always done from right to left) and pass your shuttle through the shed from right to left, leaving about two inches of wool outside the shed on the right. In throwing your weft, it should not be too slack nor should it be pulled. Draw it through so that when the shuttle comes out on the other side the weft thread will be slightly on the diagonal. Now beat it with your reed. To do this, grasp the reed in the *center* with your left hand. Even when weaving on large looms, you should use only one hand to beat, grasping the top of the reed or beater in the middle, for your hands are not equal in strength and development, and to use both hands would make one side tighter than the other. If you want a loosely woven scarf, beat only once between each shot of weft. If you want a tight weave, beat once before you change your shed and once after, before you put in the next shot of weft.

Whatever you weave, it is usual to begin with at least an inch of tabby unless your draft gives directions to the contrary.

In this scarf, however, it will be all tabby, since you have only two sheds, so, according to your taste, weave two or three inches of plain white, and then begin your color variations. This is where your imagination and creative instinct can come into play.

The great beauty of weaving is that it gives an outlet for so many of our urges, and so many varieties of temperament. The instinct for mechanical precision is gratified by the niceties of preparation to

247

weave. The actual process of weaving, throwing the shuttle back and forth, is rhythmic and repetitive, without being monotonous. There is a certain peace and serenity about it. And yet, there is always the pattern to think about, and the treadling to watch, so it never becomes dull.

When you have woven until your work gets too near the heddles to allow for a good shed, it is time to loosen the ratchets and wind the fabric onto the front roller. Leave about one inch of weaving beyond the breast beam. Then tighten up again and continue as before.

When you can no longer get a shed, you have come to the end of your warp. If you want to make something else with the same threading, prepare some more warp, and tie it on to the ends of the old warp with the weaver's knot (Fig. 14). This is much quicker, as you can readily see, than having to go through the whole process of beaming and threading again. You never tie the weft threads together, but weave them in. The way to do this is to leave a short end whenever you change your color. Then, when you change the shed, and before you throw in the next shot of weft, turn back the short end, beat it in with the rest of the work, and the place will be imperceptible.

If you are not going to "tie on" any more warp when you have finished the scarf, cut off your threads evenly, leaving enough for fringe. Pick out the first few rows of loose weaving. If you remembered, as you should have done, to jot down how much plain white tabby (minus the loose rows) you wove before you began the colored stripes, and calculated the same distance at the other end, you now have an attractive and creditable piece of work.

Now that you have had the experience of dressing a loom and of actual weaving, it will be easy for you to learn to follow designs. The illustrations on page 252 show drafts of traditional patterns. From these you can work out a great many variations with the same threadings by using different treadle combinations.

But first you must learn to read the drafts. It may look complicated, at first glance, but it is very easy. For four-harness work the drafts have five lines and four spaces, like a music staff. Each space represents a harness, and the number of each space corresponds with the number of a harness, of course. You already know that harness No. 1 is the first one toward you as you sit at the loom. It is controlled by treadle No. 1, which is the first one on the right-hand side.

For looms with more harnesses, the drafts have extra spaces. (There are other ways of notating patterns, but the one given here is commonly used now.)

After you have chosen your pattern, copy the draft. Use graph paper with good-sized squares so that you can see them quickly, or else draw up a graph yourself. Make an *exact* copy of your pattern, indicating the selvedge, and where the pattern blocks begin. Count how many threads are needed for one block.

The way to figure the number of threads for your warp is as follows: Each draft illustrated shows a complete block of the pattern. The number of "repeats" will depend upon the width of your strip. If one block has, say, 75 threads, and you want three repeats, you will need 225 threads, plus four extra at each end for selvedge and the few that you always allow for breaks or lost threads. The selvedge blocks are always lightly shaded, as you will have noticed. If you want to make a strip the whole width of your loom and your pattern blocks do not come out evenly, the way to do it is as follows: Figure out how many blocks with the selvedges you can possibly have. Count how many vacant dents this will leave. If you can make a thirty-inch strip on your loom, 15 dents to the inch, you will have to fill 450 dents. Suppose you can get eight pattern blocks of 50 threads each, allowing eight threads for selvedge, you would have 42 empty dents. You can, if you like, put in seven extra threads between every two pattern blocks threading them 1, 2, 3, 4, 3, 2, 1, and this will give you your maximum width.

For one pattern you can get a number of variations and this is possible because of the treadling, as mentioned above. Treadling is easy to understand, and a good way to master it is to select for your first pattern a small one such as the Rose Path or the Honeysuckle, and then try out all possible treadle combinations. Usually drafts give one or more treadling schemes, but when you understand it for yourself, you will be able to study a pictured design and by trying out the different sheds and noting where the weft skips over, you will be able to work out the treadling variations yourself.

As was pointed out in the description of the loom, a four-harness loom may have four treadles, one for each harness, but it may also come with six. In the former case, you will have to depress two pedals to get a shed, but in the latter case, you can tie two of the "lamms" which control the treadles together, and then use only one foot to raise two harnesses. With either four treadles, or six, you can get six different sheds on a four-harness loom, and as two of these will create your tabby, you will see that you can get patterns arising from four different treadle combinations. It works out like this:

With four treadles: 1 and 3, and 2 and 4 will be the tabby. Then you still have 1 and 2, 1 and 4, 2 and 3, and 3 and 4, making six different sheds.

249

With six treadles and a tie-up, the number of sheds will be just the same, and if you are going to work this way, decide which pedals you will keep for your tabby, and then plot out your tie-up scheme. Some weavers keep the two outside treadles for tabby, some the two end ones, either right or left. This can be at your own discretion.

The treadling for the simple Rose Path goes like this: 1 and 2, 2 and 3, 3 and 4, 4 and 1. Put a row of tabby in between each pattern shot. Remember that weaving is always from right to left, with the exception of the shuttle, which must, of course, go back and forth. Your first tabby shot will be on treadles 1 and 3. (You can think of treadling as either "lowering" or "raising," for both are true—as you lower the treadles you raise the corresponding shaft.)

When you make out the threading draft be sure to put down the treadling, then tack the graph onto the harness brace, for you will be referring to it constantly. Until you become so expert that a look at your weaving will tell you where you are and what to do next, mark down in pencil where you leave off, so that you won't make a mistake when you come back to your work.

Of course if you do put in a wrong shot, it isn't fatal or final. You can take it out again, and you will probably have to do this once in a while. If you are a true weaver you will become devoted to your craft and take a great pride in being painstaking. In a short time you will learn to go along rhythmically and smoothly and the treadling changes will sink into your consciousness and then come out in order and proper sequence. It will never become merely mechanical, though, for handloom weaving will never make a robot of you.

A good practice whenever you thread an untried pattern is to make about a yard of sampler, trying out different treadlings, and keep this in your weaving file. You can make a log book, noting down the experiments you have made and what you have found out, for you may chance on a combination that has never been recorded, and by keeping a book you will be able to reproduce it again.

After you have woven part of a pattern, if you want to see how it will look when complete, hold a mirror beyond it, and you will get the finished effect. If you are working out a treadling for yourself, this is especially helpful.

Of course, as you go on, you will devise patterns of your own. Imagination and originality, as well as a regard for good precedent, have always been characteristic of the weaving art.

If you have followed directions carefully and have checked as you have gone along, you will not run into any snags. Once in a while, however, a warp thread breaks. This is easy to remedy. If it breaks behind the harnesses, just wind a warp thread on a spool heavy

at heddle 4. But this first time, let us forget about that, and follow the rule exactly.

The first thing to do is to copy off the threading draft on a piece of stiff paper. Underneath write the treadling directions, and tack the paper up on your loom.

The simplest treadling for the Rose Path goes like this:

$$1 - 2$$
$$2 - 3$$
$$3 - 4$$
$$4 - 1$$

This means that first you lower treadles 1 and 2 (together) and put in a shot of weft. After every shot of weft you change your shed, by lowering different treadles. Between every pattern shed you put in a shot of tabby. Your tabby sheds are 1 and 3 and 2 and 4. Unless directions are given to the contrary it is taken for granted that you put in the tabby binder between every pattern shot. The way to indicate this, so that there could be no possible mistake about it would be to write your draft this way:

$$\left. \begin{array}{l} 1 - 2 \\ 2 - 3 \\ 3 - 4 \\ 4 - 1 \end{array} \right\} 1 \text{ x each, with tabby}$$

Suppose you use, for your tabby weft, beige color, and for the pattern, turquoise. You will need three shuttles—one of each color, and one with roving or rags for the first few rows, as explained before.

After you have woven in five or six rows of rag, using the tabby sheds, and remembering always to read and begin work from right to left, weave an inch or so of plain tabby with your beige weft. Then commence your pattern. It should go like this:

Lower treadles 1 and 2 — one shot turquoise weft
         1 " 3 — one shot beige tabby
         2 " 3 — one turquoise
         2 " 4 — one tabby
         3 " 4 — one turquoise
         1 " 3 — one tabby
         4 " 1 — one turquoise
         2 " 4 — one tabby

This gives you your complete pattern. Repeat this until your strip is finished.

Between each shot of weft, you "beat" your work. For close work beat once before you change your shed, and once after. Hold the batten in the middle, with *one* hand—your left will probably be more convenient.

If you want to make a sampler this first time, in order to learn more about treadling, try out a number of combinations. You can use two or three shots of weft in each shed, with binder between, for instance. Or you can reverse your pattern, and beginning with the 4-1 shed go back to the 1-2.

Here are several other Rose Path treadlings, all of them requiring the tabby binder:

1.	2.	3.
1 - 2 ⎤	3 - 4 ⎤	1 - 2 ⎤
2 - 3 ⎥	2 - 3 ⎥ 3 x	1 - 4 ⎥
3 - 4 ⎥	3 - 4 ⎰ each	1 - 2 ⎰ 2 x each
1 - 2 ⎥	1 - 4 ⎦	2 - 3 ⎦
3 - 4 ⎥		
2 - 3 ⎥	2 - 3 ⎤	1 - 4 ⎤
1 - 2 ⎥ 1 x	1 - 2 ⎥ 2 x	3 - 4 ⎥
3 - 4 ⎰ each	2 - 3 ⎰ each	1 - 4 ⎰ 1 x each
2 - 3 ⎥	3 - 4 ⎦	1 - 2 ⎦
1 - 2 ⎥		
1 - 4 ⎥	1 - 2 ⎤	3 - 4 ⎤
1 - 2 ⎥	1 - 4 ⎥ 2 x	2 - 3 ⎥
2 - 3 ⎥	1 - 2 ⎰ each	3 - 4 ⎰ 1 x each
3 - 4 ⎦	2 - 3 ⎦	1 - 4 ⎦

Try variations by using a number of colors. You could make a striped runner by using three or four colors with the first treadling and in between each block of colors have two or three inches of plain tabby.

Goose-Eye Pattern

1.		
1 - 4 ⎤		2 - 3 ⎤
3 - 4 ⎥ 1 x each and		3 - 4 ⎥
2 - 3 ⎰ repeat		1 - 4 ⎥
1 - 2 ⎦		3 - 4 ⎥ 1 x and
2.		2 - 3 ⎰ repeat
		1 - 2 ⎥
Diamond Pattern		1 - 4 ⎥
2 - 3 ⎤		3 - 4 ⎦
3 - 4 ⎥ 1 x and		
1 - 4 ⎰ repeat		2 - 3 ⎱ 1 x and
1 - 2 ⎦		1 - 2 ⎰ repeat

Honeysuckle Pattern. This is another traditional pattern, one of the most attractive of the small patterns and with dozens of different results to be arrived at by changes in treadling.

1.	**2.**	**3.**

1.

4 - 1
1 - 2 ⎫ 1 x each
2 - 3 ⎬ repeat
3 - 4 ⎭

4 - 1
3 - 4 ⎫ 1 x each
2 - 3 ⎬ repeat
1 - 2 ⎭

4 - 1
1 - 2 ⎫ 1 x each
2 - 3 ⎬ repeat
3 - 4 ⎭

4 - 1
3 - 4 ⎫ 1 x each
2 - 3 ⎭

2.

3 - 4 — 1 x
1 - 4 — 1 x
1 - 2 — 2 x
1 - 4 — 1 x
3 - 4 — 1 x
2 - 3 — 1 x
1 - 2 — 3 x
1 - 4 — 3 x
3 - 4 — 6 x
1 - 4 — 3 x
1 - 2 — 3 x
2 - 3 — 1 x

3.

3 - 4 — 1 x
1 - 4 — 1 x
1 - 2 — 2 x
2 - 3 — 2 x
3 - 4 — 3 x
1 - 4 — 6 x
3 - 4 — 3 x
2 - 3 — 2 x
1 - 2 — 2 x
1 - 4 — 1 x
2 - 3 — 1 x
1 - 2 — 3 x
2 - 3 — 1 x

4.

(Flower Design)

2 - 1 ⎫ 2 x each
4 - 1 ⎬ with tabby
2 - 1 ⎭

5.

(Leaf Design)

2 - 1 — 3 x ⎫
4 - 1 — 3 x ⎬ with
3 - 4 — 3 x ⎬ tabby
2 - 3 — 1 x ⎭

Put 12 rows of tabby between the pattern

6.	8.
(Flower All-Over Design)	(Lover's Knot) *Diamond Border*

6.	8.
2 - 1 — 3 x	4 - 1 — 3 x
4 - 1 — 3 x with	2 - 1 — 3 x
3 - 4 — 3 x tabby—	2 - 3 — 3 x
2 - 3 — 1 x reverse	2 - 1 — 3 x
2 - 1 — 4 x and	4 - 1 — 3 x
4 - 1 — 3 x repeat	3 - 4 — 3 x
2 - 1 — 4 x	
2 - 3 — 1 x	Repeat for three and
3 - 4 — 3 x	one-half inches and end
4 - 1 — 3 x	in the 2-1 heddle combina-
2 - 1 — 3 x	tion

Big Table

7.

7.	Big Table
1 - 2 — 2 x	2 - 1 — 5 x
1 - 4 — 1 x with	2 - 3 — 2 x
3 - 4 — 1 x tabby—	2 - 1 — 2 x center of square
2 - 3 — 1 x repeat from	2 - 3 — 2 x
1 - 2 — 3 x beginning	2 - 1 — 5 x
1 - 4 — 3 x	2 - 3 — 4 x
3 - 4 — 6 x	2 - 1 — 4 x
1 - 4 — 3 x	
1 - 2 — 3 x	
2 - 3 — 1 x	
3 - 4 — 1 x	
1 - 4 — 1 x	

See further variations on the following page.

Small Square or Table	Large Diamond
1 - 4 — 3 x	2 - 1 — 2 x
3 - 4 — 2 x	2 - 3 — 2 x
1 - 4 — 2 x center	3 - 4 — 2 x
3 - 4 — 2 x	4 - 1 — 2 x
1 - 4 — 3 x	3 - 4 — 2 x
	2 - 3 — 2 x
	2 - 1 — 2 x
	4 - 1 — 2 x
	3 - 4 — 2 x
	4 - 1 — 2 x
	2 - 1 — 2 x
	2 - 3 — 2 x
	3 - 4 — 2 x
	4 - 1 — 2 x
	3 - 4 — 2 x
	2 - 3 — 2 x
	2 - 1 — 2 x

CHAIR SEATS

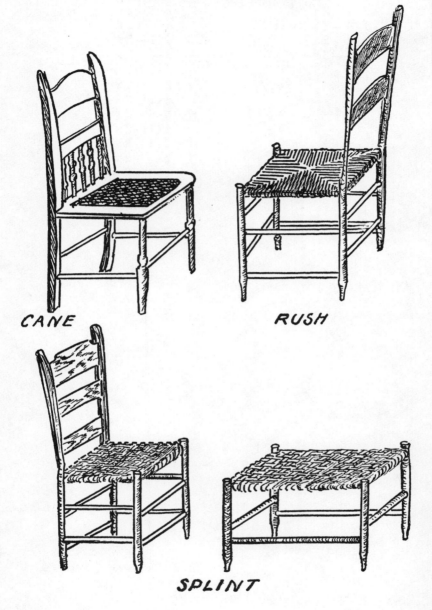

CANE

RUSH

SPLINT

CANING A CHAIR SEAT

Cane comes in hanks and can be purchased in various widths. To determine the size of cane to use, measure the holes and spaces in between. If the holes are $1/4''$ diameter and spaced $3/4''$ apart, use a medium width. Use common cane if the holes are $5/16''$ diameter and spaced $7/8''$ apart. Cut the cane into 5' to 6' lengths for working and soak strips for fifteen minutes in cold water before using.

Remove all old cane from the chair and smooth the edges. Begin the weaving by being sure all front to back strands are parallel and the side to side strands are laid in the same manner. If you are caning an irregularly shaped frame, it will be necessary to run several strands in one hole, or skip other holes, to keep the strands parallel.

To begin the operation you will need a hank of cane (one hank will cover six areas 12" by 12"), a length of binder long enough to go around the caned areas, a large-eyed heavy needle, ice pick or awl, a ruler, four 4" pegs, a sponge or cloth, and scissors or knife. The pegs, which are made pointed at one end, should be same size as holes in caning.

Begin the caning by starting at second hole at right-hand back corner (Fig. 1). Put a piece of cane into hole A and let it extend about 3" underneath frame and fasten with a peg. Next, carry it to hole B which is at the front right corner, then underneath and up through next hole C. Now carry it back to hole D and then down through D and up through E. Continue in this manner until all holes are filled. Peg at every three holes to keep cane tight while working. Be sure to keep twists out of the cane as the work is being completed.

To begin weaving a layer from side to side on top of first layer, start at second hole from left-hand back corner of side (Fig. 2). Next lay a third layer on top of second layer, making the strands parallel with the first layer (Fig. 3).

To add the fourth layer, it will be necessary to use a needle from layer to layer. The strands in this layer will be parallel to those in second layer but go under ones in first layer and over third layer. When the weaving is completed, pair the strands of first and third layers and those in second and fourth by moistening the cane and forcing together to form straight lines (Fig. 4).

You are now ready to add first layer of diagonally woven strands. Use an ice pick to force new strands down through holes. The strands go under vertical pairs and over horizontal pairs. Begin at the right-hand corner hole and weave to the one diagonally opposite. Pull through the entire length each time it is woven over and

259

CANE SEAT

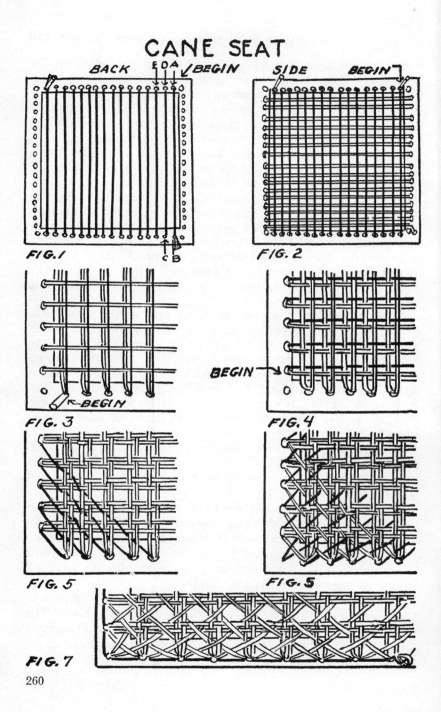

FIG. 1

FIG. 2

FIG. 3

FIG. 4

FIG. 5

FIG. 5

FIG. 7

under other strands. Work to the center, then weave the other half in the same manner (Fig. 5).

Each corner hole will have two strands of cane when chair is completed. Be sure to weave the strand diagonally across the other corner holes opposite to starting point.

Start the next layer in right-hand corner hole in back and weave the second diagonals over verticle pairs and under horizontal pairs. Twist loose ends around the loops of curved strands. (See Fig. 6.)

To finish the chair, put a strand of binder cane over holes of edges of seat (Fig. 7). Pull a strand of cane used on seat up through second or third hole from end of binder strand, then bring it over the binder and down through the same hole, then across to next one, up around binder and down. Continue until all but two or three holes under start of binder strand are bound. Overlap ends of binding cane and bend together over holes in same manner as rest of strands. When finished with last loop, plug the hole from underneath. If cane is loose in any hole, drive a small peg up through hole from under side and cut away even with chair seat. When finished and dry, coat with white shellac.

RUSH SEAT

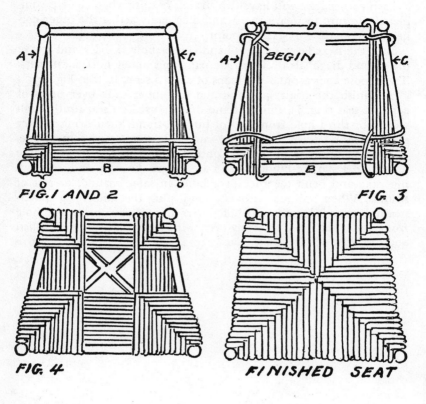

FIG. I AND 2

A→

B

C

FIG. 3

A→

BEGIN

D

B

C

FIG. 4

FINISHED SEAT

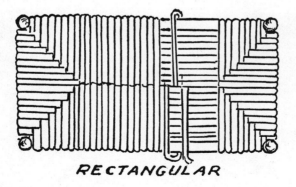

RECTANGULAR

RUSH CHAIR SEAT

To make a rush bottom for a chair you will need about two pounds of natural rush, fiber rush, or even twisted brown wrapping paper. Besides this, there will be tacks, cardboard, paper for filling between rush layers, gummed tape, a stick, a ruler, scissors, a hammer, and shellac for finishing the completed seat.

Most chair seats are wider in front than in back. To take care of this, measure off a space on the front rail equal to the length of the back rail. Have this space in the middle of the front rail, with what is left divided on each side of it (Fig. 1).

Fold end of rush and tack the strand to inner side of left side rail (A) close to front corner. Bring it over top of front rail (B) down and under front rail, over left side rail (A), then under (A) and across to side rail (C). Carry strand over top of (C), under (C), then bring it up over (B), down and tack folded end of strand to inner edge of (C) directly opposite its other end. Cut off end and continue in this way, tacking each length a little farther along on side rails (A) and (C), until spaces (O) are filled (Fig. 2). You will not need these if the back and front rails are the same length.

Make a cardboard shuttle to carry about 20 feet of your material. Fold end of strand and tack to rail. Keep splicings on underside of frame. Use a knot to splice strands. Follow Figure 3, carrying strands around all four rails.

When the seat is partly finished you will need to pack paper between the layers (see Fig. 4). Cut two triangular pieces of cardboard for each corner and fit them in. Fasten to rails with tape. Stuff shredded wrapping paper between the layers of cardboard. As you continue wrapping the seat, add stuffing. A smooth stick is best for pushing the stuffing into place.

If the seat is rectangular in shape, the short rails will be covered first. To cover the remaining area between, carry the strand over and under a long rail, across and up through center opening, then over and under the other long rail. Carry strand across and up through opening, then over and under first long rail again. Repeat this until the seat is finished. Fold end and tack to underside of rail. Two coats of thinned shellac gives a lasting finish to the seat.

REED SPLINT CHAIR SEAT OR STOOL TOP

A reed splint seat for a chair requires splints which may be ⅜″, ½″, or slightly wider if you should decide to shave out hickory splints. The splints usually come six or eight feet long. Also, you will need some heavy twine.

Soak four or five lengths of splint in warm water for about twenty minutes. While working, keep the extra splints wrapped in damp

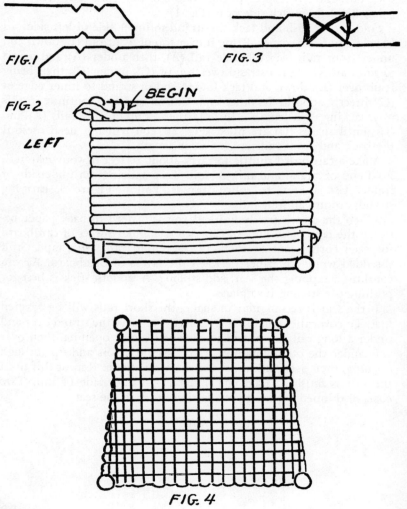

FIG. 1

FIG. 3

FIG. 2

BEGIN

LEFT

FIG. 4

newspapers. To begin, notch the end of the strip of splint (Fig. 1). At the left side of the back rail make grooves and tie end of strip here, using twine. Figure 2 shows the beginning wrap. Work from left to right around a seat. Bring strip under, then up around left-side rail, across seat, then down and under right-side rail. Carry strip across seat and up around left rail and across to right. Continue wrapping from side to side until area is covered by warp strips. Be sure to keep smooth surface of splints on upper side, and do not wrap the warp strings too tightly or there will be no place for the weavers. The weavers go under and over the warp splints. Tie the end to the under side of the rail. Notch the end and groove the rail as you did to begin.

When you need to take a new splint, be sure the jointure comes on the underside. Lay two strips together and tie as shown in Figure 3.

To start weaving, attach end of new length of splint to back rail at right side, as first end was attached. Weave, using over and under weave, from back to front. Weave underside of seat too. Continue until corresponding sections of back and front rail are filled. If the seat is the same width at the back as at the front, this completes the weaving, but the seats are usually wider at the front (see Fig. 4).

To weave any ends in, run strip under warp strips on underside, then turn sharply back and tuck end under two strips. Next, weave open spaces on each side of front rail, start on underside in front and after tapering a short length of splint, push under weave at bottom, bring other end around front rail to top and weave across to back of seat. Trim ends and push back under work just completed. Repeat with as many pieces as necessary on each side to fill openings. Make sure that there are the same number of extra strips on each side.

When finished weaving, notch and tie ends together under seat. Thinned shellac gives a durable finish to the splints. They may be stained or colored with a mixture of turpentine, linseed oil, and your choice of oil paint. Shellac is used over this.

INDEXES

Alphabetical Index

269

Functional Index

SECONDARY
    Cement Sculpture
    Chair Caning
    Etched Jewelry
    Indian Crafts
    Leather Carving
    Leathercraft
    Making a Sundial
    Metalcraft
    Nature Prints

Plastics
Poster Ideas
Pottery
Puppets
Spatter Printing
Stenciling
Weaving
Whittling
Woodworking
Woven Bracelets

LITTLE CHILDREN

The craft projects suggested for young children can be created from materials found in any household. They are designed to stimulate interest in nature, dramatics, and other activities.

Box Toys
Cardboard Furniture
Corn Cob Dolls
Child's Flower Garden
Doll House
Feltograms
Finger Painting
Flower Dolls
Indian Crafts
Nature Prints

Newspaper Doll
Outdoor Play Equipment
Paper Bag Puppets
Paper Modeling
Pillow Puppets
Play Store
Scrap Lumber Project
Susie-Bur-Rabbit
Uses for Crayons
Wooden Dolls

HOME CRAFTS

Each member of the family will find many crafts he will want to make. The following are a few that fit the needs of every home:

Appliqué
Caning Chairs
Corn Husk Articles
Decorating Tin
Decorating Trays
Doll House
Jewelry
Laying on Gold Leaf
Leather Sandals
Pottery

Quilting
Refinishing Antique Chairs
Refinishing Furniture
Rug Making
Spatter Printing
Spinning
Stenciling
Toys
Weaving

TEEN-AGERS

Many crafts in this book will satisfy the teen-ager both as an individual and as a group activity for his club. We suggest:

Camp Equipment
Cement Sculpture
Christmas Decorations
Decorating Trays
Etched Jewelry
Furniture Decorations
Leathercraft
Novel Belts
Party Decorations

Plastics
Poster Ideas
Pottery
Properties for Dramatics
Puppets
Sandals
Stenciling
Weaving
Woodworking

274

GIRLS' CLUBS

Girls working in groups such as Girl Scouts, YWCA, Campfire Girls, 4-H Clubs, can find crafts to make the year around. Here are some that are most useful:

Appliqué
Basketry
Bead Craft
Christmas Decorations
Corn Husk Articles
Jewelry Making
Leathercraft
Metalcraft
Nature Prints
Party Decorations

Pottery
Puppets
Spatter Printing
Spinning
Stenciling
Tie Dyeing
Useful Bags
Weaving
Woodworking

BOYS' CLUBS

Boys that participate in club programs such as Boy Scouts, YMCA, Boys' Clubs of America, will find the following crafts most interesting:

Caning Chairs
Cement Sculpture
Indian Crafts
Jewelry
Lashing
Leathercraft
Making a Sundial
Metalcraft
Mobiles

Nature Prints
Outdoor Cooking Equipment
Plastics
Poster Ideas
Pottery
Puppet Making
Refinishing Furniture
Toys
Woodworking

CHURCHES

Church members of all ages will find suggestions for making articles that can be used in the yearly bazaar.

Appliqué
Articles from Natural Materials
Basketry
Christmas Decorations
Crafts for Little Children
Dolls
Hooked Rugs
Jewelry
Leathercraft
Luncheon Sets

Metalcraft
Party Decorations
Plastics
Poster Ideas
Puppets
Quilting
Refinishing Furniture
Spatter Printing
Useful Bags

A CATALOGUE OF SELECTED DOVER BOOKS
IN ALL FIELDS OF INTEREST

A CATALOGUE OF SELECTED DOVER BOOKS
IN ALL FIELDS OF INTEREST

THE NOTEBOOKS OF LEONARDO DA VINCI, edited by J.P. Richter. Extracts from manuscripts reveal great genius; on painting, sculpture, anatomy, sciences, geography, etc. Both Italian and English. 186 ms. pages reproduced, plus 500 additional drawings, including studies for Last Supper, Sforza monument, etc. 860pp. 7⁷/₈ x 10¾. USO 22572-0, 22573-9 Pa., Two vol. set $12.00

ART NOUVEAU DESIGNS IN COLOR, Alphonse Mucha, Maurice Verneuil, Georges Auriol. Full-color reproduction of Combinaisons ornamentales (c. 1900) by Art Nouveau masters. Floral, animal, geometric, interlacings, swashes — borders, frames, spots — all incredibly beautiful. 60 plates, hundreds of designs. 9³/₈ x 8¹/₁₆. 22885-1 Pa. $4.00

GRAPHIC WORKS OF ODILON REDON. All great fantastic lithographs, etchings, engravings, drawings, 209 in all. Monsters, Huysmans, still life work, etc. Introduction by Alfred Werner. 209pp. 9¹/₈ x 12¼. 21996-8 Pa. $6.00

EXOTIC FLORAL PATTERNS IN COLOR, E.-A. Seguy. Incredibly beautiful full-color pochoir work by great French designer of 20's. Complete Bouquets et frondaisons, Suggestions pour étoffes. Richness must be seen to be believed. 40 plates containing 120 patterns. 80pp. 9³/₈ x 12¼. 23041-4 Pa. $6.00

SELECTED ETCHINGS OF JAMES A. McN. WHISTLER, James A. McN. Whistler. 149 outstanding etchings by the great American artist, including selections from the Thames set and two Venice sets, the complete French set, and many individual prints. Introduction and explanatory note on each print by Maria Naylor. 157pp. 9³/₈ x 12¼. 23194-1 Pa. $5.00

VISUAL ILLUSIONS: THEIR CAUSES, CHARACTERISTICS, AND APPLICATIONS, Matthew Luckiesh. Thorough description, discussion; shape and size, color, motion; natural illusion. Uses in art and industry. 100 illustrations. 252pp. 21530-X Pa. $2.50

TEN BOOKS ON ARCHITECTURE, Vitruvius. The most important book ever written on architecture. Early Roman aesthetics, technology, classical orders, site selection, all other aspects. Stands behind everything since. Morgan translation. 331pp. 20645-9 Pa. $3.50

THE CODEX NUTTALL. A PICTURE MANUSCRIPT FROM ANCIENT MEXICO, as first edited by Zelia Nuttall. Only inexpensive edition, in full color, of a pre-Columbian Mexican (Mixtec) book. 88 color plates show kings, gods, heroes, temples, sacrifices. New explanatory, historical introduction by Arthur G. Miller. 96pp. 11³/₈ x 8½. 23168-2 Pa. $7.50

THE MAGIC MOVING PICTURE BOOK, Bliss, Sands & Co. The pictures in this book move! Volcanoes erupt, a house burns, a serpentine dancer wiggles her way through a number. By using a specially ruled acetate screen provided, you can obtain these and 15 other startling effects. Originally "The Motograph Moving Picture Book." 32pp. 8¼ x 11. 23224-7 Pa. $1.75

STRING FIGURES AND HOW TO MAKE THEM, Caroline F. Jayne. Fullest, clearest instructions on string figures from around world: Eskimo, Navajo, Lapp, Europe, more. Cats cradle, moving spear, lightning, stars. Introduction by A.C. Haddon. 950 illustrations. 407pp. 20152-X Pa. $3.50

PAPER FOLDING FOR BEGINNERS, William D. Murray and Francis J. Rigney. Clearest book on market for making origami sail boats, roosters, frogs that move legs, cups, bonbon boxes. 40 projects. More than 275 illustrations. Photographs. 94pp. 20713-7 Pa. $1.25

INDIAN SIGN LANGUAGE, William Tomkins. Over 525 signs developed by Sioux, Blackfoot, Cheyenne, Arapahoe and other tribes. Written instructions and diagrams: how to make words, construct sentences. Also 290 pictographs of Sioux and Ojibway tribes. 111pp. 6⅛ x 9¼. 22029-X Pa. $1.50

BOOMERANGS: HOW TO MAKE AND THROW THEM, Bernard S. Mason. Easy to make and throw, dozens of designs: cross-stick, pinwheel, boomabird, tumblestick, Australian curved stick boomerang. Complete throwing instructions. All safe. 99pp. 23028-7 Pa. $1.75

25 KITES THAT FLY, Leslie Hunt. Full, easy to follow instructions for kites made from inexpensive materials. Many novelties. Reeling, raising, designing your own. 70 illustrations. 110pp. 22550-X Pa. $1.25

TRICKS AND GAMES ON THE POOL TABLE, Fred Herrmann. 79 tricks and games, some solitaires, some for 2 or more players, some competitive; mystifying shots and throws, unusual carom, tricks involving cork, coins, a hat, more. 77 figures. 95pp. 21814-7 Pa. $1.25

WOODCRAFT AND CAMPING, Bernard S. Mason. How to make a quick emergency shelter, select woods that will burn immediately, make do with limited supplies, etc. Also making many things out of wood, rawhide, bark, at camp. Formerly titled Woodcraft. 295 illustrations. 580pp. 21951-8 Pa. $4.00

AN INTRODUCTION TO CHESS MOVES AND TACTICS SIMPLY EXPLAINED, Leonard Barden. Informal intermediate introduction: reasons for moves, tactics, openings, traps, positional play, endgame. Isolates patterns. 102pp. USO 21210-6 Pa. $1.35

LASKER'S MANUAL OF CHESS, Dr. Emanuel Lasker. Great world champion offers very thorough coverage of all aspects of chess. Combinations, position play, openings, endgame, aesthetics of chess, philosophy of struggle, much more. Filled with analyzed games. 390pp. 20640-8 Pa. $4.00

DECORATIVE ALPHABETS AND INITIALS, edited by Alexander Nesbitt. 91 complete alphabets (medieval to modern), 3924 decorative initials, including Victorian novelty and Art Nouveau. 192pp. 7¾ x 10¾. 20544-4 Pa. $4.00

CALLIGRAPHY, Arthur Baker. Over 100 original alphabets from the hand of our greatest living calligrapher: simple, bold, fine-line, richly ornamented, etc. — all strikingly original and different, a fusion of many influences and styles. 155pp. 11⅜ x 8¼. 22895-9 Pa. $4.50

MONOGRAMS AND ALPHABETIC DEVICES, edited by Hayward and Blanche Cirker. Over 2500 combinations, names, crests in very varied styles: script engraving, ornate Victorian, simple Roman, and many others. 226pp. 8⅛ x 11. 22330-2 Pa. $5.00

THE BOOK OF SIGNS, Rudolf Koch. Famed German type designer renders 493 symbols: religious, alchemical, imperial, runes, property marks, etc. Timeless. 104pp. 6⅛ x 9¼. 20162-7 Pa. $1.75

200 DECORATIVE TITLE PAGES, edited by Alexander Nesbitt. 1478 to late 1920's. Baskerville, Dürer, Beardsley, W. Morris, Pyle, many others in most varied techniques. For posters, programs, other uses. 222pp. 8⅜ x 11¼. 21264-5 Pa. $5.00

DICTIONARY OF AMERICAN PORTRAITS, edited by Hayward and Blanche Cirker. 4000 important Americans, earliest times to 1905, mostly in clear line. Politicians, writers, soldiers, scientists, inventors, industrialists, Indians, Blacks, women, outlaws, etc. Identificatory information. 756pp. 9¼ x 12¾. 21823-6 Clothbd. $30.00

ART FORMS IN NATURE, Ernst Haeckel. Multitude of strangely beautiful natural forms: Radiolaria, Foraminifera, jellyfishes, fungi, turtles, bats, etc. All 100 plates of the 19th century evolutionist's Kunstformen der Natur (1904). 100pp. 9⅜ x 12¼. 22987-4 Pa. $4.00

DECOUPAGE: THE BIG PICTURE SOURCEBOOK, Eleanor Rawlings. Make hundreds of beautiful objects, over 550 florals, animals, letters, shells, period costumes, frames, etc. selected by foremost practitioner. Printed on one side of page. 8 color plates. Instructions. 176pp. 9³/₁₆ x 12¼. 23182-8 Pa. $5.00

AMERICAN FOLK DECORATION, Jean Lipman, Eve Meulendyke. Thorough coverage of all aspects of wood, tin, leather, paper, cloth decoration — scapes, humans, trees, flowers, geometrics — and how to make them. Full instructions. 233 illustrations, 5 in color. 163pp. 8⅜ x 11¼. 22217-9 Pa. $3.95

WHITTLING AND WOODCARVING, E.J. Tangerman. Best book on market; clear, full. If you can cut a potato, you can carve toys, puzzles, chains, caricatures, masks, patterns, frames, decorate surfaces, etc. Also covers serious wood sculpture. Over 200 photos. 293pp. 20965-2 Pa. $3.00

EGYPTIAN MAGIC, E.A. Wallis Budge. Foremost Egyptologist, curator at British Museum, on charms, curses, amulets, doll magic, transformations, control of demons, deific appearances, feats of great magicians. Many texts cited. 19 illustrations. 234pp. USO 22681-6 Pa. $2.50

THE LEYDEN PAPYRUS: AN EGYPTIAN MAGICAL BOOK, edited by F. Ll. Griffith, Herbert Thompson. Egyptian sorcerer's manual contains scores of spells: sex magic of various sorts, occult information, evoking visions, removing evil magic, etc. Transliteration faces translation. 207pp. 22994-7 Pa. $2.50

THE MALLEUS MALEFICARUM OF KRAMER AND SPRENGER, translated, edited by Montague Summers. Full text of most important witchhunter's "Bible," used by both Catholics and Protestants. Theory of witches, manifestations, remedies, etc. Indispensable to serious student. 278pp. 6⅝ x 10. USO 22802-9 Pa. $3.95

LOST CONTINENTS, L. Sprague de Camp. Great science-fiction author, finest, fullest study: Atlantis, Lemuria, Mu, Hyperborea, etc. Lost Tribes, Irish in pre-Columbian America, root races; in history, literature, art, occultism. Necessary to everyone concerned with theme. 17 illustrations. 348pp. 22668-9 Pa. $3.50

THE COMPLETE BOOKS OF CHARLES FORT, Charles Fort. Book of the Damned, Lo!, Wild Talents, New Lands. Greatest compilation of data: celestial appearances, flying saucers, falls of frogs, strange disappearances, inexplicable data not recognized by science. Inexhaustible, painstakingly documented. Do not confuse with modern charlatanry. Introduction by Damon Knight. Total of 1126pp.
23094-5 Clothbd. $15.00

FADS AND FALLACIES IN THE NAME OF SCIENCE, Martin Gardner. Fair, witty appraisal of cranks and quacks of science: Atlantis, Lemuria, flat earth, Velikovsky, orgone energy, Bridey Murphy, medical fads, etc. 373pp. 20394-8 Pa. $3.50

HOAXES, Curtis D. MacDougall. Unbelievably rich account of great hoaxes: Locke's moon hoax, Shakespearean forgeries, Loch Ness monster, Disumbrationist school of art, dozens more; also psychology of hoaxing. 54 illustrations. 338pp. 20465-0 Pa. $3.50

THE GENTLE ART OF MAKING ENEMIES, James A.M. Whistler. Greatest wit of his day deflates Wilde, Ruskin, Swinburne; strikes back at inane critics, exhibitions. Highly readable classic of impressionist revolution by great painter. Introduction by Alfred Werner. 334pp. 21875-9 Pa. $4.00

THE BOOK OF TEA, Kakuzo Okakura. Minor classic of the Orient: entertaining, charming explanation, interpretation of traditional Japanese culture in terms of tea ceremony. Edited by E.F. Bleiler. Total of 94pp. 20070-1 Pa. $1.25